# WHAT EVERY SPECIAL EDUCATOR MUST KNOW

## THE INTERNATIONAL STANDARDS FOR THE PREPARATION AND LICENSURE OF SPECIAL EDUCATORS

**Third Edition**
**1998**

**The Council for Exceptional Children**

Library of Congress Cataloging-in-Publication Data

The Council for Exceptional Children
        What every special educator must know: The international standards for the preparation and
    licensure of special educators. --
    3rd ed.
    p.    cm.
    Includes bibliographical references (p.    ).
    Stock no. R5277" -- T.p. verso.
    ISBN 0-86586-323-7  (pbk.)
    1. Special education teachers--Training of--Standards.   2.Special education teachers--Certification--Stan-
    dards.   I. Title.
    LC3969.45.C69   1998
    379.1'57--dc21
                                                                                    98-45480
                                                                                    CIP


Copyright 1998 by the Council for Exceptional Children, 1920 Association Drive, Reston, Virginia 20191-1589

Stock No. R5277

Printed in the United States of America

10  9  8  7  6  5  4  3  2  1

**One of the original aims of CEC:**

**. . . to establish professional standards for teachers**

**in the field of special education.**

First CEC meeting, 1923

**The quality of educational services for children and youth**

**with exceptionalities resides in the abilities, qualifications,**

**and competencies of the personnel who provide the**

**services.**

CEC, 1988

# Table of Contents

## *Appendices*

# *Preface*

*It was through significant professional and personal commitment that the members of CEC crafted this product. In the process we learned not only about knowledge and skills but also about each other and developed a deep mutual respect. May those who use this [publication] experience that same mutual respect from all who serve children and their families.*

Preamble to the Common Core, 2nd edition

*What Every Special Educator Must Know: The International Standards for the Preparation and Licensure of Special Educators* is intended to provide the kind of leadership and guidance that makes us proud to be special educators.

- For students preparing to become special educators, this publication will introduce you to the ethics and professional practice standards to which you aspire. It describes the knowledge and skills which will be the foundation of your professional practice.

- For teachers, you will not only find your professional ethics, practice standards, and your professional standards, you will also find guidance in developing a plan for your continuing professional growth.

- For professors and deans developing or revising your programs, you will find the procedures for seeking national recognition of your programs either through the National Council for Accreditation of Teacher Education (NCATE) and CEC or through CEC alone. It is our sincere hope that many of you will find the new Curriculum Referenced Licensing and Program Accreditation Framework helpful in preparing your programs for national recognition.

- For state directors and specialists, you will find guidance for revising state licensing standards to align with the profession's recommendations. CEC stands ready to assist you in this process.

- For parents and others from the community, you will find the ethics, professional practice standards, and the knowledge and skills that we, as the special education profession, use to define ourselves and judge each others excellence.

# Introduction

There exists today a constellation of factors that shape the reform of public education in America, and as corollary the reform of special education. Report after report describes the need to do better. Schools have raised the bar. Children are taking more rigorous courses. Students, schools, and teachers are facing increased accountability. General and special educators are recognizing that collaboration and mutual problem-solving are critical. Students with exceptionalities are accessing the general education curriculum in numbers only dreamed of just a few years ago. Schools are learning to include students with exceptionalities in assessment programs and reporting the results in ways that are useful for program improvement.

However, whether in special or general education classrooms, it is clear that the single most important influence in the education of children is the teacher. The widely respected report from The National Commission on Teaching and America's Future, *What Matters Most: Teaching for America's Future* is based on three assumptions:

- What teachers know and can do is the most important influence on what a student learns.
- Recruiting, preparing, and retaining good teachers is the central strategy for improving our schools.
- School reform cannot succeed unless it focuses on creating the conditions in which teachers can teach, and teach well.

As the international association of special education professionals, The Council for Exceptional Children (CEC) embraces the responsibility to provide leadership in the development, revision, and implementation of standards for the special education profession. Just as our profession grows and learns so must the standards and knowledge base grow and respond to new knowledge. This publication is the 3rd edition of the profession's standards.

The reader will find several changes in this edition including:

- The Curriculum Referenced Licensing and Program Accreditation Framework that was approved in the spring of 1998 is included.

- Eleven items were added to the Common Core Knowledge and Skill Standards.

- Several newly approved sets of Knowledge and Skill Standards have been included: Special Education Administrator, Educational Diagnostician, Transition Specialist, and Special Education Paraeducator.

Like its predecessors, this edition is a collaborative product of the members of CEC and others in the wider educational community. The standards and principles represent the expertise and ideas of literally thousands of special educators. This effort is based on the premises that:

- Professional standards must come from the profession itself.
- Special education is an international profession, not limited to a single state, province, or location.

The standards provide to states, provinces, and nations benchmarks for developing or revising policy and procedures for program accreditation, entry level licensure, professional practice, and continuing professional growth.

As we approach the millennium, the development and implementation of professional standards for the field of special education remains one of the most important responsibilities of CEC. For three quarters of a century, CEC has provided the leadership for professional standards, giving voice to the profession through its membership. Over the years, as knowledge, practice, and theory advanced, CEC has responded by regularly updating its standards. CEC maintains professional standards for:

- Professional practice.
- Entry into the profession and continuing professional growth.
- Preparation programs.

## Section 1. Standards for Professional Practice

Central to any profession is its will to abide by a set of ethical principles and standards. As professionals serving individuals with exceptionalities, special educators possess a special trust endowed by the community. As such, special educators have a responsibility to be guided by their professional principles and practice standards.

Section 1 contains the CEC Code of Ethics and Standards for Professional Practice. The **Code of Ethics** is eight fundamental ethical premises to which all special educators are bound. The **Standards for Professional Practice** describe the principles special educators use in carrying out day-to-day responsibilities. The Professional Practice Standards are how special educators are measured and in turn measure each other's professional excellence. It is incumbent on all special educators to use these standards in all aspects of their professional practice.

### Section 2. Standards for Entry Into the Profession and for Continuing Professional Growth.

This section contains the standards and recommendations of the profession regarding licensure and certification. While licensure is the prerogative and responsibility of the state or province in which the professional chooses to practice, it is the responsibility of the profession to provide guidance and leadership to state licensing authorities. It is through this dialogue, that states ensure that the special educators they license possess the knowledge and skills validated by practicing professionals.

CEC is pleased to share for the first time in this edition the **Curriculum Referenced Licensing and Program Accreditation Framework** recommended for licensing of entry level professionals in special education whenever the state or province is seeking a multicategorical licensure. In addition, for the first time the Guidelines for Mentoring and for Continuing Practice in the Profession are also included.

### Section 3. CEC International Standards for Special Education Professional Preparation Programs

In 1976, CEC and the National Council for Accreditation of Teacher Education (NCATE) began an important partnership. NCATE is responsible for the national accreditation of colleges of education nationally. As NCATE's partner for special education programs, CEC is responsible for nationally recognizing quality special education preparation programs. Special education preparation programs from across the United States submit their programs for national accreditation and recognition by NCATE and CEC.

Students considering a special education career should verify that the programs they are considering are both NCATE and CEC approved. The most di-

rect way to ensure that the program prepares students using the profession's validated knowledge and skills is to select a college or university that is NCATE approved and CEC recognized.

This section contains the knowledge and skill standards that special education preparation programs use for developing and evaluating their programs and that CEC uses for the national accreditation process.

### Section 4. CEC Knowledge and Skill Standards for Beginning Special Educators

This section contains the profession's Knowledge and Skill Standards. They provide the basis for the curriculum that colleges and universities use to prepare special educators. In addition, these sets or groups of Knowledge and Skill Standards are used by states and provinces to establish entry level licensing standards in special education.

CEC continues to update the knowledge and skill standards as the field develops. One example is the **curriculum referenced licensing and program accreditation framework** that was approved in the spring of 1998. While retaining the knowledge and skills in the exceptionality/age specific category sets, it has become clear that CEC must provide active leadership to states and provinces that are seeking the profession's guidance for preparing and licensing special educators for multicategorical practice. The knowledge and skill standards in the Curriculum Referenced Licensing and Program Accreditation Framework provides this guidance.

The framework will be useful to college/university level special education preparation programs in both program development and program accreditation. Moreover, this framework will be useful to states in aligning their licensure requirements with the profession's knowledge and skill bases. Significantly, for many states this will provide a framework that can be used to align state and national standards in coordinating licensure and program accreditation.

The revisions of the common core knowledge and skill standards are included in this edition along with new knowledge and skill standards for:

- Paraeducators serving students with exceptionalities,
- Career/transition specialists,
- Educational diagnosticians, and
- Special education administrators.

CEC is currently developing knowledge and skill standards for special education technology specialists. Areas under development currently include skills and knowledge needed by all special educators in the areas of technology, general education curriculum, diversity, and collaborative teaching.

## *Appendices*

There are several appendices that may be of interest to readers. Appendix 1 is a brief summary of events in the history of special education and professional standards. Appendix 2 contains a brief history of the development of the CEC Standards and the procedures that CEC uses for on-going development and validation of the Knowledge and Skill Standards. Appendix 3 is the reprint of an article from *TEACHING Exceptional Children* that gives a narrative history of professional standards in special education. Appendix 4 is a self-evaluation instrument designed to be used by students of special education to evaluate their progress in learning the knowledge and skills they will need upon graduation from the preparation program.

# Section 1
## CEC Code of Ethics and Standards for Professional Practice for Special Educators

### CEC CODE OF ETHICS FOR EDUCATORS OF PERSONS WITH EXCEPTIONALITIES

We declare the following principles to be the Code of Ethics for educators of persons with exceptionalities. Members of the special education profession are responsible for upholding and advancing these principles. Members of The Council for Exceptional Children agree to judge and be judged by them in accordance with the spirit and provisions of this Code.

Special Education Professionals:

A. Are committed to developing the highest educational and quality of life potential of individuals with exceptionalities.

B. Promote and maintain a high level of competence and integrity in practicing their profession.

C. Engage in professional activities which benefit individuals with exceptionalities, their families, other colleagues, students, or research subjects.

D. Exercise objective professional judgment in the practice of their profession.

E. Strive to advance their knowledge and skills regarding the education of individuals with exceptionalities.

F. Work within the standards and policies of their profession.

G. Seek to uphold and improve where necessary the laws, regulations, and policies governing the delivery of special education and related services and the practice of their profession.

H. Do not condone or participate in unethical or illegal acts, nor violate professional standards adopted by the Delegate Assembly of CEC.

### CEC STANDARDS FOR PROFESSIONAL PRACTICE

#### Professionals in Relation to Persons with Exceptionalities and Their Families

#### Instructional Responsibilities

Special education personnel are committed to the application of professional expertise to ensure the provision of quality education for all individuals with exceptionalities. Professionals strive to:

(1) Identify and use instructional methods and curricula that are appropriate to their area of professional practice and effective in meeting the individual needs of persons with exceptionalities.

(2) Participate in the selection and use of appropriate instructional materials, equipment, supplies, and other resources needed in the effective practice of their profession.

(3) Create safe and effective learning environments which contribute to fulfillment of needs, stimulation of learning, and self-concept.

(4) Maintain class size and case loads which are conducive to meeting the individual instructional needs of individuals with exceptionalities.

(5) Use assessment instruments and procedures that do not discriminate against persons with exceptionalities on the basis of race, color, creed, sex, national origin, age, political practices, family or social background, sexual orientation, or exceptionality.

(6) Base grading, promotion, graduation, and/or movement out of the program on the individual goals and objectives for individuals with exceptionalities.

(7) Provide accurate program data to administrators, colleagues, and parents, based on efficient and objective record keeping practices, for the purpose of decision making.

(8) Maintain confidentiality of information except when information is released under specific conditions of written consent and statutory confidentiality requirements.

## Management of Behavior

Special education professionals participate with other professionals and with parents in an interdisciplinary effort in the management of behavior. Professionals:

(1) Apply only those disciplinary methods and behavioral procedures which they have been instructed to use and which do not undermine the dignity of the individual or the basic human rights of persons with exceptionalities, such as corporal punishment.

(2) Clearly specify the goals and objectives for behavior management practices in the persons' with exceptionalities Individualized Education Program.

(3) Conform to policies, statutes, and rules established by state/provincial and local agencies relating to judicious application of disciplinary methods and behavioral procedures.

(4) Take adequate measures to discourage, prevent, and intervene when a colleague's behavior is perceived as being detrimental to exceptional students.

(5) Refrain from aversive techniques unless repeated trials of other methods have failed and only after consultation with parents and appropriate agency officials.

## Support Procedures

(1) Adequate instruction and supervision shall be provided to professionals before they are required to perform support services for which they have not been prepared previously.

(2) Professionals may administer medication, where state/provincial policies do not preclude such action, if qualified to do so or if written instructions are on file which state the purpose of the medication, the conditions under which it may be administered, possible side effects, the physicians name and phone number, and the professional liability if a mistake is made. The professional will not be required to administer medication.

(3) Professionals note and report to those concerned whenever changes in behavior occur in conjunction with the administration of medication or at any other time.

## Parent Relationships

Professionals seek to develop relationships with parents based on mutual respect for their roles in achieving benefits for the exceptional person. Special education professionals:

(1) Develop effective communication with parents, avoiding technical terminology, using the primary language of the home, and other modes of communication when appropriate.

(2) Seek and use parents' knowledge and expertise in planning, conducting, and evaluating special education and related services for persons with exceptionalities.

(3) Maintain communication between parents and professionals with appropriate respect for privacy and confidentiality.

(4) Extend opportunities for parent education utilizing accurate information and professional methods.

(5) Inform parents of the educational rights of their children and of any proposed or actual practices which violate those rights.

(6) Recognize and respect cultural diversities which exist in some families with persons with exceptionalities.

(7) Recognize that the relationship of home and community environmental conditions affects the behavior and outlook of the exceptional person.

## Advocacy

Special education professionals serve as advocates for exceptional students by speaking, writing, and acting in a variety of situations on their behalf. They:

(1) Continually seek to improve government provisions for the education of persons with exceptionalities while ensuring that public statements by professionals as individuals are not construed to represent official policy statements of the agency that employs them.

(2) Work cooperatively with and encourage other professionals to improve the provision of special education and related services to persons with exceptionalities.

(3) Document and objectively report to ones supervisors or administrators inadequacies in resources and promote appropriate corrective action.

(4) Monitor for inappropriate placements in special education and intervene at appropriate

levels to correct the condition when such inappropriate placements exist.

(5) Follow local, state/provincial, and federal laws and regulations which mandate a free appropriate public education to exceptional students and the protection of the rights of persons with exceptionalities to equal opportunities in our society.

## Professional in Relation to Employment

### Certification and Qualification

Professionals ensure that only persons deemed qualified by having met state/provincial minimum standards are employed as teachers, administrators, and related service providers for individuals with exceptionalities.

### Employment

(1) Professionals do not discriminate in hiring on the basis of race, color, creed, sex, national origin, age, political practices, family or social background, sexual orientation, or exceptionality.

(2) Professionals represent themselves in an ethical and legal manner in regard to their training and experience when seeking new employment.

(3) Professionals give notice consistent with local education agency policies when intending to leave employment.

(4) Professionals adhere to the conditions of a contract or terms of an appointment in the setting where they practice.

(5) Professionals released from employment are entitled to a written explanation of the reasons for termination and to fair and impartial due process procedures.

(6) Special education professionals share equitably the opportunities and benefits (salary, working conditions, facilities, and other resources) of other professionals in the school system.

(7) Professionals seek assistance, including the services of other professionals, in instances where personal problems threaten to interfere with their job performance.

(8) Professionals respond objectively when requested to evaluate applicants seeking employment.

(9) Professionals have the right and responsibility to resolve professional problems by utilizing established procedures, including grievance procedures, when appropriate.

### Assignment and Role

(1) Professionals should receive clear written communication of all duties and responsibilities, including those which are prescribed as conditions of their employment.

(2) Professionals promote educational quality and intra- and interprofessional cooperation through active participation in the planning, policy development, management, and evaluation of the special education program and the education program at large so that programs remain responsive to the changing needs of persons with exceptionalities.

(3) Professionals practice only in areas of exceptionality, at age levels, and in program models for which they are prepared by their training and/or experience.

(4) Adequate supervision of and support for special education professionals is provided by other professionals qualified by their training and experience in the area of concern.

(5) The administration and supervision of special education professionals provides for clear lines of accountability.

(6) The unavailability of substitute teachers or support personnel, including aides, does not result in the denial of special education services to a greater degree than to that of other educational programs.

### Professional Development

(1) Special education professionals systematically advance their knowledge and skills in order to maintain a high level of competence and response to the changing needs of persons with exceptionalities by pursuing a program of continuing education including but not limited to participation in such activities as inservice training, professional conferences/workshops, professional meetings, continuing education courses, and the reading of professional literature.

(2) Professionals participate in the objective and systematic evaluation of themselves, colleagues, services, and programs for the purpose of continuous improvement of professional performance.

(3) Professionals in administrative positions support and facilitate professional development.

## Professionals in Relation to the Profession and to Other Professionals

### The Profession

(1) Special education professionals assume responsibility for participation in professional organizations and adherence to the standards and codes of ethics of those organizations.

(2) Special education professionals have a responsibility to provide varied and exemplary supervised field experiences for persons in undergraduate and graduate preparation programs.

(3) Special education professionals refrain from using professional relationships with students and parents for personal advantage.

(4) Special education professionals take an active position in the regulation of the profession through use of appropriate procedures for bringing about changes.

(5) Special education professionals initiate, support, and/or participate in research related to the education of persons with exceptionalities with the aim of improving the quality of educational services, increasing the accountability of programs, and generally benefiting persons with exceptionalities. They:

- Adopt procedures that protect the rights and welfare of subjects participating in the research.
- Interpret and publish research results with accuracy and a high quality of scholarship.
- Support a cessation of the use of any research procedure which may result in undesirable consequences for the participant.
- Exercise all possible precautions to prevent misapplication or misuse of a research effort, by self or others.

### Other Professionals

Special education professionals function as members of interdisciplinary teams, and the reputation of the profession resides with them. They:

(1) Recognize and acknowledge the competencies and expertise of members representing other disciplines as well as those of members in their own disciplines.

(2) Strive to develop positive attitudes among other professionals toward persons with exceptionalities, representing them with an objective regard for their possibilities and their limitations as persons in a democratic society.

(3) Cooperate with other agencies involved in serving persons with exceptionalities through such activities as the planning and coordination of information exchanges, service delivery, evaluation, and training, to avoid duplication or loss in quality of services.

(4) Provide consultation and assistance, where appropriate, to both general and special educators as well as other school personnel serving persons with exceptionalities.

(5) Provide consultation and assistance, where appropriate, to professionals in nonschool settings serving persons with exceptionalities.

(6) Maintain effective interpersonal relations with colleagues and other professionals, helping them to develop and maintain positive and accurate perceptions about the special education profession.

# CEC International Standards for Entry Into Professional Practice and for Continuing Professional Growth

*The education of teachers must be driven by*

- *a clear and careful conception of the educating we expect our schools to do,*
- *the conditions most conducive to this educating (as well as conditions that get in the way), and*
- *the kinds of expectations that teachers must be prepared to meet.*

*Goodlad, 1990*

Today educators teach an increasing complex and diverse population of students. Within special education also, students with exceptionalities continue to challenge us to respond to their complex and diverse needs. They call us to address them not simply as students with disabilities, but as students with families, cultures, communities, and other complex needs. Along with our general education colleagues, special educators are actively building approaches and structures that are effective and responsive to the realities of our students.

The questions regarding how special educators are prepared and how they are licensed are closely related to assuring a quality cadre of teachers. The relationship between the accreditation of programs that prepare special educators and licensing of special educators must be strong and direct. CEC has embraced the responsibility to provide leadership in the development, revision, and implementation of standards for the special education profession. For over 75 years, CEC has led the special education profession in this responsibility. Over the years literally thousands of CEC members have contributed their time and skills to enable CEC to carry on this responsibility.

As a part of this responsibility, CEC has stipulated standards for both entry to the profession and for continuing practice in the profession. In addition to providing the basis for national certification through the Professionally Recognized

Special Educator National Certification Program, these standards are intended as guidance to state, provincial, and national agencies and bodies responsible for licensing special educators to practice in their jurisdictions.

### Entry Into Professional Practice

To be qualified to initial entry into practice as a special educator an individual must:

1. *possess no less than a bachelor's degree;*
2. *have the knowledge and skills set forth in the CEC **Common Core** of Knowledge and Skills Essential for All Beginning Special Education Teachers; and,*
3. *have the knowledge and skills set forth in the **Areas of Specialization** for which the individual seeks to practice.*

The standards make clear that entry level special educators will, at a minimum, possess a bachelor's degree, along with having the knowledge and skills delineated by the profession. First of all, all special educators need the CEC Common Core of Knowledge and Skills Essential for All Beginning Special Education Teachers. However, the Common Core is not a set of knowledge and skills needed to teach students with mild exceptionalities.

The special educator must also have the knowledge and skills set forth in the Areas of Specialization for which the individual seeks license to practice. In other words, if the special educator is licensed to teach students with varying exceptionalities, then the special educator should possess the knowledge and skills to teach each of those exceptionalities. (See Figure 1.) The real challenge in multicategorical licensure lies not in diluting the preparation, but in preparing individuals with the knowledge and skills needed to teach students with a variety of exceptionalities.

In the past, there has been an erroneous perception that CEC's approach to licensing and program accreditation was strictly categorical. CEC has never had a policy that either licensure or program accreditation be categorical. In order to clarify this perception and, more importantly, to offer active leadership and guidance to the field, CEC has developed a curriculum referenced licensing and program accreditation framework. (See Figure 2.)

### The Curriculum Referenced Licensure and Accreditation Framework

Currently, the majority of states and provinces license special educators to serve students with a variety of disabilities. Over 20 separate titles are used to describe some variant of a multicategorical license. The types of disabilities included by each are even more variable. While the titles of licenses and the categories of disabilities of students included in the frameworks differ, the trend has been toward two major licensing categories: special education teachers of students with mild/moderate disabilities and special education teachers of students with severe/profound disabilities. A major drawback of this approach is that it simply changes from referencing disabilities to referencing groups of disabilities.

The CEC Curriculum Referenced Licensing and Program Accreditation Framework uses curriculum to structure the two major components of the framework: one for special education teachers of students with disabilities who are most likely to make progress in an individualized general curriculum (See Section 4, p. 119) and the other for special education teachers of students who are most likely to make progress in an individualized independence curriculum (See Section 4, p. 126). This CEC Curriculum Referenced Licensing and Program Accreditation Framework retains many of the strengths of the disability-referenced approach while avoiding many of the controversies regarding the divisions of mild, moderate, severe, and profound. It is also in consonance with the focus on curriculum delineated in IDEA 97 (Public Law 105-17).

Moreover, for state and provincial program accreditation most colleges and universities prepare program folios in conformance with state and provincial certification, and state and provincial program evaluation requirements. Even in those states and provinces that have retained categorical certification, market forces provide strong encouragement to colleges and universities to provide programs preparing special educators to educate students with a variety of disabilities.

The CEC Curriculum Referenced Licensing and Program Accreditation Framework provides guidance to state and provincial licensing agencies regarding the profession's recommendation for a licensing framework that is multicategorical. Colleges and universities will find preparing accreditation folios clearer and more direct because the CEC Curriculum Referenced Licensing and Program Accreditation Framework will very likely be more in coordination with the types of programs offered.

The CEC Curriculum Referenced Licensing and Program Accreditation Framework is intended to encourage consensus and alignment in both accreditation and state and provincial licensure frameworks. However, states and provinces frequently have unique requirements influenced by local needs or legislated requirements. Recognizing this reality, the indexing of items to each area of specialization will facilitate the customization of items in line with unique state and provincial requirements.

In developing the CEC Curriculum Referenced Licensing and Program Accreditation Framework, the Knowledge and Skills Subcommittee took great care to guard the body of CEC validated knowledge and skills in the specialization areas. Essentially, each knowledge and skill was reviewed by the Subcommittee to determine where, not whether, it should be included in the framework. Many items fit and were entered in both the individualized general curriculum standards and the individualized independence curriculum standards. Wherever appropriate to reduce duplication and to increase ease of reading, the subcommittee edited items together. However, each edited knowledge or skill is clearly indexed to the unedited items.

This allows the user to track the inclusion of each item in a specific training program.

Programs preparing special education teachers of students accessing an individualized general curriculum include the relevant knowledge and skills from the following categorical specialization areas:

- Students with Learning Disabilities.
- Students with Emotional and Behavioral Disorders.
- Students with Physical and Health Disabilities.
- Students with Mental Retardation and Developmental Disabilities.

Programs preparing special education teachers of students accessing an individualized independence curriculum, include the relevant knowledge and skills from the following categorical specialization areas:

- Students with Learning Disabilities.
- Students with Emotional and Behavioral Disorders.
- Students with Physical and Health Disabilities.
- Students with Mental Retardation and Developmental Disabilities.

The subcommittee included a number of knowledge and skills from the Deaf and Hard of Hearing and Visual Impairments Areas of Specialization. More and more children with sensory impairments are being served in the general curricula and settings with special education services in collaboration with resource teachers and teachers of students with visual impairments or of students who are deaf or hard of hearing. It is important that entry level special educators have the knowledge and skills to work in collaboration with these and other specialists.

## Mentorship

*In addition, each new professional in special education should receive a minimum of a 1-year mentorship during the first year of professional special education practice. The mentor should be an experienced professional in the same or a similar role as the mentee who can provide expertise and support on a continuing basis.*

Even with quality preparation, the beginning special educator faces new challenges in applying and generalizing new skills and knowledge. Like other professionals, special educators who have the support of more senior colleagues become proficient more quickly, and are more likely to remain in the profession. The goals of the mentorship program should include:

- facilitating the application of knowledge and skills learned;
- conveying advanced knowledge and skills;
- acculturating into the school's learning community;
- reducing job stress and enhancing job satisfaction; and
- supporting professional induction.

When special educators begin practice in a new area of licensure, they should have the opportunity to work with mentors who are experienced professionals in similar roles. The purpose of mentors is to provide expertise and support to the teachers on a continuing basis for at least the first year of practice in that area of certification. The mentorship is part of continuing education; thus, it is a requirement for maintaining licensure, not a requirement for initial licensure.

The mentorship is a professional relationship between the new teacher and an experienced teacher that aids the new teacher in further developing knowledge and skills in the area of certification and provides the support required to sustain the new teacher in practice. The mentorship is collegial, not supervisory. It is essential that a mentor have knowledge, skills, and experience relevant to the new teacher's position in order to provide the expertise and support the new teacher requires to practice effectively. Thus, it is essential that new teachers practice in environments where mentors are available. Members of the special education profession are expected to serve as mentors as part of their professional responsibilities, and they should receive the resources and support necessary to carry out this responsibility effectively.

The CEC Standards provide that special education teachers should receive mentorships when they begin practice in each area of licensure. Thus, for example, an experienced teacher of students with visual impairments who, after the necessary preparation, becomes licensed to teach students in early childhood should receive a mentorship during the first year of practice in early childhood in order to maintain the license in early childhood.

### Continuing Practice in the Profession

*Both state licensure and national certification of individuals for professional practice in the field of special education should be for a limited period of time with periodic renewal. Each professional in the field of educating individuals with exceptionalities shall participate in an average of 36 contact hours (or an average of 3.6 continuing education units) each year of planned, organized, and recognized professional development activities related to the professional's field of practice.*

The day has passed when one can assume that they have mastered a job and no longer need new skills. Today the average worker will change careers at least three times in their work life. And even within the same career, essential skills are changing at a dramatic rate. Just 10 years ago, many teachers saw technology skills as peripheral to their jobs.

Just as teachers in general must be lifelong learners, so too must special educators pursue new knowledge and skills throughout their careers. Licensure or certification must be time limited, and renewal must be based on planned, organized, and recognized professional development activities related to the professional's field of practice.

CEC has approved the following guidelines to implement the continuing practice standard.

Each professional shall have a Professional Development Plan (PDP) that meets the standard and guidelines.

- Activities used in the PDP to earn continuing education units (CEU) can be selected from the following categories: career related academic course work, conducting or supporting research, participating in inservice workshops, teaching courses, delivering presentations, publishing, participating in supervised collegial support, providing service to professional association(s), participating in approved educational travel, and other appropriate projects.
- The PDP is reviewed and amended at least annually.
- Activities in the PDP are above and beyond routine job functions of the professional, and no single activity or category makes up the plan.
- The PDP includes an average of 3.6 CEUs per year.
- CEUs are earned in at least 3 of past 5 years.

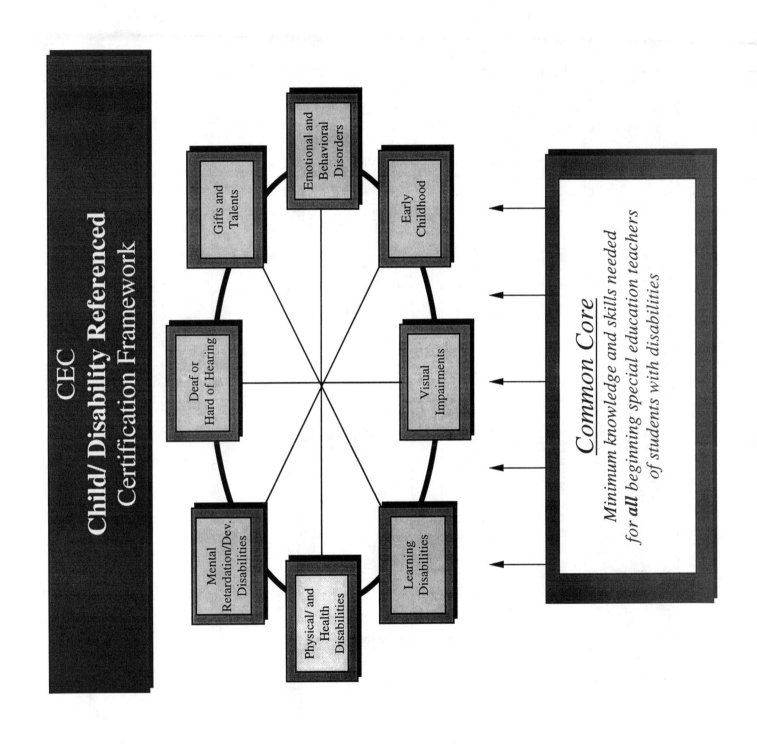

# CEC
# Child/Disability Referenced Certification Framework

Emotional and Behavioral Disorders

Gifts and Talents

Early Childhood

Deaf or Hard of Hearing

Visual Impairments

Mental Retardation/Dev. Disabilities

Physical/ and Health Disabilities

Learning Disabilities

*Common Core*
Minimum knowledge and skills needed for **all** beginning special education teachers of students with disabilities

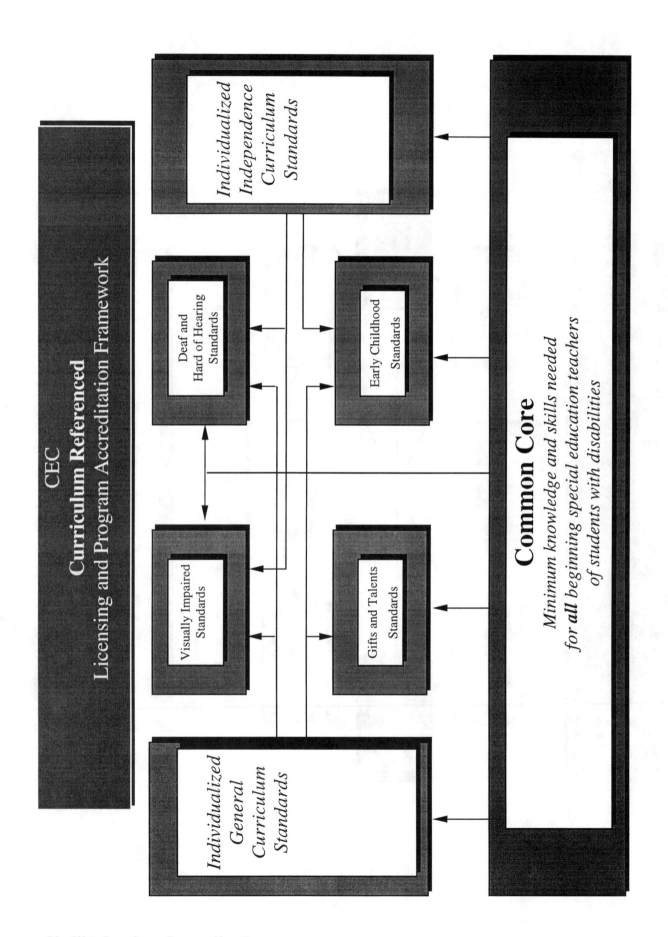

CEC
**Curriculum Referenced**
Licensing and Program Accreditation Framework

Individualized Independence Curriculum Standards

Deaf and Hard of Hearing Standards

Early Childhood Standards

Visually Impaired Standards

Gifts and Talents Standards

Individualized General Curriculum Standards

**Common Core**
*Minimum knowledge and skills needed for **all** beginning special education teachers of students with disabilities*

It is incumbent on colleges and universities that prepare special education professionals to do so in a manner consistent with the standards of the profession. All special education programs in colleges and universities should be approved by CEC. In addition, all professional education preparation programs in the United States should be accredited by the National Council for accreditation of Teacher Education (NCATE). The Guidelines included in this section are used by CEC to evaluate special education professional preparation programs to determine whether or not such programs meet CEC's Standards for Special Education Professional Preparation Programs.

CEC has two options for program approval. First, a college or university that is seeking accreditation through NCATE submits its special education program to NCATE for CEC review. Second, a college or university may apply directly to CEC for review of its special education program outside of the NCATE process.

### Procedures for Programs Seeking CEC Approval Through NCATE

In 1976, CEC and NCATE began an important partnership. Under this arrangement, NCATE is responsible for accreditation of the overall teacher education unit, (e.g., the college of education). As NCATE's partner for special education, CEC is responsible for nationally recognizing quality special education preparation programs within the teacher education unit.

An Institution of Higher Education (IHE) that is seeking accreditation from NCATE receives a publication titled *NCATE Curriculum Guidelines* from NCATE. This notebook includes the guidelines for initial and advanced programs in special education. These curriculum guidelines, prepared by CEC, contain the CEC Guidelines for Approval of Special Education Professional Preparation Programs except for those requirements that are assessed by NCATE through the evaluation of the overall teacher ed-

ucation unit. Details on all necessary information required for folio completion, as well as all the necessary forms, are found only in the NCATE Curriculum Guidelines available from NCATE.

It is expected that special education faculty take part in continuous self-study of their special education programs. Based upon this assessment, faculty prepare a folio that provides evidence that the special education programs meet all of the requirements set forth in the Guidelines.

The folio is then sent to NCATE, who in turn, sends it to CEC. At CEC, a panel of trained field reviewers evaluates the folio. For each guideline, panelists verify whether the evidence provided is sufficient to demonstrate that the program meets the requirement.

Based upon this assessment, CEC prepares a report outlining the reviewers decision including the basis for that determination. CEC sends a copy of the report to the IHE and to NCATE. If the program is not approved, the IHE may then submit a rejoinder to NCATE providing clarification or additional evidence. The rejoinder is reviewed and a second determination is made and communicated to the IHE and to NCATE. The IHE may continue to repeat the process until it is resolved.

CEC at times approves programs that substantially meet the Guidelines with the understanding that specified improvements will be instituted within a specified time period.

### Procedures for Programs Seeking CEC Accreditation Outside of the NCATE Process

From time to time, CEC receives requests for program recognition directly from a college or university that is outside of the NCATE process. CEC has developed procedures for direct review and program recognition when requested.

IHEs seeking accreditation directly through CEC, without going through NCATE, should request a copy of the CEC Special Education Preparation Program Accreditation Procedures packet from CEC. This packet will contain all the necessary forms, guidelines, and deadlines that the IHE will need to prepare a folio.

It is expected that special education faculty take part in continuous self-study of their special education programs. Based upon this assessment, faculty prepare a folio that provides evidence that the special education programs meet all of the requirements set forth in the CEC Special Education Preparation Program Accreditation Procedures.

The folio is then sent to CEC. At CEC, a panel of trained field reviewers evaluates the folio. For each guideline, panelists verify whether the evidence provided is sufficient to demonstrate that the program meets the requirement.

CEC next prepares a report regarding whether or not the program is conditionally approved, along with the basis of the determination. CEC sends a copy of the report to the IHE. If the program is not approved, the IHE may submit a rejoinder providing clarification or additional information. The rejoinder is reviewed and a second determination is made and communicated to the IHE. The IHE may continue to repeat the process until it is resolved.

After the folio approval, a field team of evaluators conducts a site visit to the IHE to validate the information that was provided in the folio. Based on their recommendations, CEC informs the IHE of its decision regarding approval of its special education programs.

### Development of the CEC Guidelines

In 1983 the CEC Delegate Assembly adopted CEC Standards for the Preparation of Special Education Personnel. Based on these Standards, CEC developed CEC/NCATE Guidelines for CEC Program Approval of Undergraduate or Basic Programs and CEC/NCATE Guidelines for CEC Program Approval of Graduate or Advanced Programs. These Guidelines were adopted by NCATE in 1985 and were revised in 1991.

In 1992, CEC adopted the CEC Common Core of Knowledge and Skills Essential for All Beginning Special Education Teachers. In subsequent years, the Subcommittee on Knowledge and Skills began developing specialty sets of knowledge and skills to supplement the Common Core. (For a complete description of the development of the CEC Standards, see Part 2.) The

Accreditation Subcommittee of the Professional Standards and Practice Standing Committee incorporated the Common Core and Area of Specialization knowledge and skills into the CEC accreditation standards. In 1996, after initial publication, comments were received from the field regarding the knowledge and skills statements and the institutional and program requirements. After review of all of the comments, CEC approved in the spring of 1996 a number of technical and clarifying changes. These are included in this edition. The relevant portions of the guidelines were submitted to NCATE for review and approved in 1996.

CEC submits its standards to NCATE for review every 5 years. CEC's next review will be in 2001. At that time, CEC will submit standards that have been developed since 1996, including Educational Diagnosis, Special Education Administration, and Technology Specialist. Although, these have not yet been approved by NCATE, it is recommended that institutions seeking approval for these programs use the CEC standards in these areas.

In 1992 CEC adopted Non-NCATE Guidelines for Program Approval for Institutions of Higher Education that wanted CEC approval of their special education programs but did not choose to seek NCATE accreditation. These include guidelines for the institution, for faculty, for program resources, etc. These Guidelines were amended in 1993.

## Institutional and Program Standards

Institutions seeking accreditation directly through CEC must meet all of the following requirements. Those institutions seeking accreditation through NCATE must respond to items 1 through 4 under the General Special Education Program Information Standards and all items under the Area of Specialization Standards. Please note that there is information necessary to complete a NCATE folio not contained in these requirements. Details on all necessary information required for folio completion are found in the *NCATE Curriculum Guidelines* available from NCATE.

### Institutional Standards

1. The institution in which the special education program is housed is accredited by the appropriate institutional accrediting agencies.

2. The institution in which the special education program is housed is an equal opportunity employer that does not discriminate on the basis of race, sex, color, religion, age, or disability (consistent with Section 702 of Title VII of the 1964 Civil Rights Act, which deals with exemptions for religious corporations, with respect to employment of individuals with specific religious convictions).

### General Special Education Program Information Standards

1. The special education program maintains procedures for continuing interaction with consumers (graduates, school systems, teachers, and organizations).
2. Multicultural issues are integrated throughout the program.
3. The institution maintains a process for developing the curriculum for the preparation of special education personnel that includes procedures for the study of the recommendations of national professional organizations (e.g., CEC, CEC divisions, American Speech-Language-Hearing Association, American Nursing Association, National Association for the Education of Young Children) as they may affect special education programs.
4. Practicum Standards
   - Field experiences are sequential in difficulty.
   - Each field experience has clearly stated, measurable objectives that relate to the overall goals and objectives of the program.
   - The field experiences involve model professionals (e.g., teachers, early interventionists) who use practices congruent with the knowledge and skills expected of the student candidate.
   - Cooperating professionals are provided guidelines that structure field experiences.
   - The student teaching experience is in the same type of settings as that for which the student candidate is seeking licensure/certification.
   - The student teaching experience is with the same type of individuals as those with whom the candidate is preparing to work.
   - Candidates are placed only with cooperating professionals who are appropriately licensed/certified in the specialization in which candidates are seeking certification.
   - Each area of specialization provides supervision to candidates by university/college faculty qualified and experienced in teaching in the area of specialization.
   - During student teaching, the supervisor from the university/college observes the candidate at least five times.
   - Explicit performance criteria are established for student teaching and each field experience.
   - Students have a minimum of 10 full-time weeks or the equivalent clock-hour composite (e.g., 350 clock hours) of supervised practicum/student teaching in the areas of specialization for which the candidate is being prepared.
   - Knowledge and Skills required for each practicum experience reflect "recommended practices."
   - Practicum experiences are supervised under a structured program of advisement.
   - Each area of specialization has responsibility for assigning candidates to approved placements. This responsibility includes the approval of cooperating teachers and supervisors. Criteria for the selection and retention of such persons are in writing and subject to ongoing evaluation.
   - Each area of specialization has written criteria for the selection and retention of cooperating professionals and supervisors.
5. Resources available to support an effective special education professional preparation program:
   - The budget trends for the special education programs over the past 5 years and future planning indicate continued support for special education programs.
   - Special education facilities are accessible to individuals with disabilities.
   - The special education program allocates its available resources to programs in a manner that allows each of them to meet its mission and needs.
   - Modern equipment is available to support administration, research, service, and instructional needs of the special education program.
   - Financial support provided during the last 5 years has been adequate for instructional materials and technology.

- Library holdings provide adequate scope, breadth, and currency to support the special education program.
- An identifiable and relevant media and materials collection is accessible to special education students and faculty.
- Systematic reviews of library and media materials are conducted periodically and are used to make acquisitions decisions by the special education program.
- Necessary supplies are provided to support special education faculty, students, staff, and administration in the operation and implementation of programs, policies, and procedures.

6. Maintaining an effective special education faculty:
   - The teaching load of undergraduate special education faculty is no more than the equivalent of 12 semester/quarter hours, and the teaching load of graduate special education faculty is no more than the equivalent of 9 semester/quarter hours.
   - Faculty work load assignments accommodate faculty involvement in teaching, scholarship, and service.
   - Instructional resources for supervision of special education practicum experiences do not exceed a ratio of 18 full-time equivalent students to one full-time equivalent faculty member.
   - The use of part-time faculty and graduate students who teach in special education programs is limited to prevent the fragmentation of instruction and the erosion of quality, and they are supervised by full-time faculty to ensure program integrity, quality, and continuity.
   - Special education faculty view themselves as members of the training and research arms of the teaching profession.
   - Special education faculty are actively involved in professional associations and professional activities at the local, state, national, and/or international levels in their areas of expertise and assignment.
   - The special education faculty are regularly involved with the professional world of practice at the appropriate level of instruction (infant, toddler, preschool, elementary, and/or secondary).

- Systematic faculty development activities are provided for faculty, cooperating teachers, and others who may contribute to special education programs.
- Support for special education faculty development is at least at the level of that for other units in the institution.
- Faculty keep abreast of developing work and debates about research on teaching and special education, as well as recent scholarly work in the areas that they teach.
- Special education faculty are regularly evaluated in terms of their contributions to the areas of teaching, scholarship, and service. These evaluation data are used in determining salary, promotion, and tenure.
- Competence in teaching is evaluated through direct measures of teaching effectiveness such as student evaluations.
- Evaluations of special education faculty are systematically used to improve teaching, scholarly and creative activities, and service within the program.

7. Student recruitment, selection, and support:
   - Applicants from diverse economic, racial, and cultural backgrounds and individuals with disabilities are recruited.
   - Incentives and affirmative procedures are used to attract high-quality candidates who represent a culturally diverse population and individuals with disabilities.
   - Special education students have access to publications that describe program standards and institutional policies, including clear statements of due process.
   - The special education program's advisory system provides special education students access to academic and professional assistance, including information about standards needed to complete their special education programs.
   - Special education students are made aware of the availability of social and psychological counseling services within the institution.

8. Relationship to the community and local schools:
   - The special education program and local schools, early intervention settings, and agencies cooperatively develop research questions and inquiry strategies to encourage the involvement of practicing profes-

sionals with the special education faculty for further development and refinement of the professional knowledge bases.

- Positive working relationships with local schools are developed and maintained to improve the delivery of high-quality education in the schools, early intervention settings, and agencies.
- The special education program has developed arrangements with school districts, early intervention settings, and agencies in its geographical area.

### Area of Specialization Program Standards

1. The area of specialization program provides students with each of the knowledge and skills set forth in the CEC Common Core of Knowledge and Skills Essential for All Beginning Special Education Teachers. (See Matrix, pp. 21-27.)
2. The area of specialization program provides students with each of the knowledge and skills set forth in the appropriate CEC Specialized Knowledge and Skills Essential for Beginning Special Education Teachers. (See Matrix, pp. 29-92. Note: If an institution's specialization program covers more than one of CEC's specialization areas, then either a separate matrix is required for each specialization covered or the institution can use one of the curriculum referenced matrices, pp. 29-38)

For specializations other than those covered by the CEC Specialized Knowledge and Skills Essential for Beginning Special Education Teachers, the program has developed required knowledge and skills.

### Advanced Program Standards:

- The course work is advanced in nature and meets the institution's criteria for advanced studies.
- No more than one third of the advanced courses are open to undergraduates.
- Each advanced program includes the study of research methods and findings, the students are knowledgeable consumers of research data, and graduates are prepared to engage in research activities.

### FREQUENTLY ASKED QUESTIONS ABOUT CEC ACCREDITATION PROCEDURES

*Do these Guidelines apply to programs administered outside the special education unit?*

Yes. These guidelines are for all programs that prepare professionals in the education of children with exceptionalities without regard to where they are housed in the college or university. For example, some early childhood special education and gifted and talented programs are located outside the special education unit. These programs should complete the appropriate requirements and be submitted as part of the total folio.

*What are some of the benefits IHEs and their students receive from going through the program approval process?*

Some of the benefits include the following:

- Most IHEs that have gone through the process report that it helped them clarify and improve their programs.
- Lists of approved programs are published by CEC and disseminated to the CEC membership and individuals seeking information about special education professional preparation programs.
- Approved programs are cited in the Directory of Programs for Preparing Individuals for Careers in Special Education published by CEC.
- CEC provides the special education program with a certificate indicating that the program meets the professional standards of CEC.
- Certificates are available for students who graduate from approved programs stating that they have graduated from a CEC-approved professional preparation program.
- It is assumed that graduates from approved programs will have met the basic requirements for CEC's certification standards for entry into special education practice.

*Do the CEC Guidelines constitute the totality of a high-quality special education professional preparation program?*

No, CEC Guidelines are a minimum. They are designed to establish a common set of professional expectations among all professional preparation programs and the profession. We believe that high-quality programs build upon that floor using unique talents of the faculty, students, and other professionals in the community to teach the continually emerging knowledge derived from research and practice.

*The Standards define the knowledge and skills a special education teacher should have. However, as the preamble to the Common Core notes, "It is assumed that a special educator who is required to teach specific subjects or content areas . . . has additional preparation, practicum experiences, and expertise in those areas."*

CEC does not advocate any one model (e.g., competency-based) for teacher preparation programs. Although listings of competencies or knowledge and skills may appear to support one type of model, this is not CEC's intention. Instead, the knowledge and skills statements should be viewed as minimum requirements, with an expectation that IHEs will extend their program development and refinement.

*Do the Guidelines define what a special educator should know and be able to do to perform at a level of excellence in the profession?*

No. The Guidelines define the minimum essential knowledge and skills necessary for entry into practice. The CEC members who developed these Guidelines recognized that there are many things that need to be learned through practice and continuing education. All special educators are expected to continually upgrade their knowledge and skills through planned, preapproved, organized, and recognized professional development activities. The CEC International Standards for Entry Into Professional Practice also state that "employing agencies should provide resources to enable each professional's continuing development."

*How should an IHE approach using and meeting CEC's Practicum Standards?*

High-quality practicum experiences are an essential part of any effective professional preparation program. It is through practicum experiences that students preparing for future professional roles practice and demonstrate the skills they must have to perform these roles. Thus, it is expected that the practicum experiences align with the knowledge and skills requirements in the common core and the areas of specialization. For example: Early Childhood Special Educators are prepared to provide family-centered services; thus, these practicum experiences should include opportunities to practice and demonstrate skills in this area.

CEC recognizes that there are a variety of approaches to providing practicum experiences that can be utilized to meet the varying needs of students, colleges and universities, and practicum sites. The Guidelines focus on the qualitative components of the practicum, rather than a model. The Guidelines do require that students have a minimum of 10 full-time weeks or the equivalent clock-hour composite of supervised practicum experience in the areas of specialization for which they are being prepared. If a candidate is being prepared to teach more than one area of specialization it is expected that within the 10-week practicum the student will have the opportunity to practice and demonstrate the skills required across the varying specializations for which he or she is being prepared.

*Most of the Area of Specialization Guidelines are by category of exceptionality. Is CEC promoting exceptionality specific professional preparation programs?*

No. CEC does not advocate any one model for teacher preparation programs. However, IHEs must accommodate their particular state's licensure framework. For over 45 states, this includes some form of multicategorical special education licensure—but no states define these in the same way. This has made it very difficult for CEC to provide a single multicategorical framework to meet all of these needs. In response to this situation, CEC provides two options for universities dealing with these issues.

The first is for the university to provide CEC with a description of the students their teachers are being prepared to serve, and then complete the appropriate matrices. For example, a university that has a Mild/Moderate program could define that as preparing teachers to work with students who have learning disabilities and mental retardation. The IHE would then complete the Common Core, Learning Disabilities, and Mental Retardation matrices to demonstrate that it is preparing teachers with mastery of the knowledge and skills in both areas of specialization.

A second option is provided by the new Curriculum Referenced Framework, included for the first time in this edition of *What Every Special Educator Must Know*. The framework uses curriculum to structure the two major components. The framework contains two matrices, each of which can be used separately (with the Common Core). The first matrix contains standards for special education teachers who are working with individuals with disabilities who are most likely to make progress in an individualized general curriculum. The second matrix contains standards for special education teachers working with individuals with disabilities who are most likely to make progress in an independence living curriculum. (For a complete description of the Alternative Framework, see Section 2.)

### What percentage of IHEs submitting folios to CEC receive CEC approval of their programs?

The present rate of program approval is approximately 80%.

### What if a college or university has areas of specialization that are not among the areas of specialization developed by CEC?

These programs should still be submitted for review. It is expected that the program submission will include all of the requirements set forth in the Area of Specialization Program Standards and the CEC Common Core of Knowledge and Skills Essential for All Beginning Special Education Teachers. In addition, the program should articulate the role definition of those completing the program and the knowledge and skills necessary to carry out that role. The knowledge and skills should be organized in the same groups as in the Common Core knowledge and skills.

If the program is preparing individuals for careers other than teaching (e.g., special education administration) and the IHE assumes that the students already possess the Common Core of Knowledge and Skills Essential for All Beginning Special Education Teachers, then the information submitted should include documentation of such requirements in the IHEs admission standards.

### Are there programs in colleges and universities that should not be submitted for CEC review?

The CEC Guidelines and review process are designed to evaluate programs that prepare individuals for various professional roles in special education for example, careers in special education teaching, supervision, administration, professional preparation, research and others. However, IHEs often offer programs in continuing education that enhance knowledge and skills but do not specifically prepare the student for entry into a professional role. CEC is not currently in a position to review such programs. Likewise, CEC does not review preparation programs that do not result in certification.

### Will CEC approve programs accredited by ASHA?

CEC recognizes the standards of other professional associations when those standards meet the basic requirements of our standards. After a review of the Accreditation Standards of the American Speech-Language-Hearing Association (ASHA), CEC's Professional Standards and Practice Standing Committee determined that CEC should approve speech pathology and audiology programs that have been accredited by ASHA's Educational Standards Board. In the same manner, CEC has agreed to approve those preparation programs accredited by the Council on the Education of the Deaf (CED) when those programs have met CED approval based on the standards approved by CED in 1998. Programs approved by these organizations need only to submit to CEC their letter of accreditation for CEC recognition.

### Will these Standards change over time?

CEC recognizes that what we need to know to practice effectively changes with advances in research and practice and that any standards will need to be updated over time. Therefore, the CEC Professional Standards and Practice Standing Committee has established a process for the continual monitoring and improvement of these Standards and consideration of amendments offered by members and CEC units. A description of this process can be found in Appendix 3.

### What assistance is available from CEC to assist IHEs seeking CEC program approval?

CEC's goal is to have all special education professional preparation programs meet our Guidelines. Thus, we view assisting IHEs through the folio process and helping them improve their programs as essential parts of the process. Among the various forms of assistance CEC offers are the following:

*Instructional Manual for Preparing Folios to Meet CEC/NCATE Special Education Guidelines* [publication expected in January 1999] Folio training for programs: One-day writers' workshops offered at various times and sites throughout the year. For a list of upcoming training dates, check the CEC web site (http://www.cec.sped.org).

On-site training: CEC staff are available to conduct 1-day writers' workshops with special education faculty on campus.

Technical assistance: CEC staff are available to answer E-mail and telephone inquiries.

For further information, please call 703/264-9484, TTY 703/264-9446, FAX 703/264-1637, E-mail address: cecprof@CEC.sped.org.

# Section 4
# CEC Knowledge and Skill Standards for Beginning Special Educators

The matrices included in this chapter are the Knowledge and Skill Standards that have been validated by the profession. They are used by colleges and universities to ensure that special education preparation programs align with the knowledge and skill base of the profession. They are also used by states and provinces in assuring the public that the special educators they license possess the knowledge and skills of their profession. This section includes the CEC Common Core, the CEC Curriculum-Referenced Standards, the CEC Area of Specialization Standards, and the CEC Standards for Educational Diagnosticians, Special Education Administrators, Transition Specialists, and Special Education Paraeducators.

The sets of Knowledge and Skill Standards define only essential entry level knowledge and skills. As such they are minimal standards. All special educators are expected to continuously upgrade their knowledge and skills through planned, organized, and recognized professional development activities.

The Knowledge and Skill Standards in the Common Core represent the knowledge and skills base that every special educator must possess. It is on this base that areas of specialization are added, leading to the initial entry of the individual into the profession. Special educators who practice in a specific area(s) of special education must possess the appropriate Areas of Specialization Knowledge and Skills adopted by CEC in addition to the Common Core.

The Knowledge and Skills Standards define the knowledge and skills directly relevant to special education. There are skills and knowledge that all general educators must possess to be able to work in collaboration with special educators with students with exceptionalities. Likewise, special educators must possess a working knowledge of the general education curriculum to work in collaboration with their general education colleagues.

It is assumed that special educators who teach specific general education curriculum subjects or content (e.g., science, social studies, foreign languages, vocational education) have appropriate additional preparation and experience in these areas.

In addition, special education has within its heritage the perspectives of advocacy for persons with exceptionalities and of embracing individual differences. These differences include the traditional considerations of the nature and effect of exceptionalities. As the community of exceptional children, youth, and adults has become increasingly diverse, these perspectives have broadened to include other characteristics that significantly influence their quality of life.

In order to advocate for their multicultural clients, special educators today must have a broad perspective to ensure vigilant attention to the issues of diversity. Current demographic trends clearly indicate that:

- The numbers of children and youth from culturally and linguistically diverse backgrounds served in public schools are growing rapidly.
- Cultural and linguistic diversity is expected to continue to increase.
- The number of professionals who are culturally and linguistically diverse entering the special education profession has been declining even as the numbers of students who are culturally and linguistically diverse are rising.

Given the pervasive nature of diversity, professional standards need to guide professional practice in ways that are relevant to the multicultural populations served in special education. Specifically, these standards reflect the premise that, to design effective interventions, special educators must understand the characteristics of the learners they serve, including factors such as culture, language, gender, religion, and sexuality.

This premise has been addressed in two ways. First, the Knowledge and Skill Standards are inclusive in nature; that is, they identify knowledge and skills essential to effectively serve all exceptional learners, including those from culturally and linguistically diverse backgrounds. Second, selected items address the most critical aspects of diversity and are infused throughout the standards.

Moreover, the sustained involvement of families, colleagues in general education, and the larger community is fundamental to delivering high-quality educational services to individuals with exceptional learning needs. The knowledge and skills contained in this document should be interpreted to include learners of all ages, beginning with infants and preschoolers and extending to young adults who are transitioning from school programs. Similarly, the term families should be interpreted broadly to include biological mothers and fathers, adoptive parents, legal guardians, foster parents or primary caregivers, siblings, and extended family members. In addition, it is assumed that special educators may provide learning opportunities in a variety of learning environments, including the home, preschool, school, and community settings, as well as in both specialized and integrated environments.

Finally, the sets of Knowledge and Skill Standards are built on the assumption that the professional conduct of entry-level special educators is governed foremost by the CEC Code of Ethics and Professional Practice Standards.

# CEC Common Core of Knowledge and Skills Essential for All Beginning Special Education Teachers

## KNOWLEDGE AND SKILLS STATEMENTS

### CC: Common Core
### 1. Philosophical, Historical, and Legal Foundations of Special Education

*Knowledge:*

K1 Models, theories, and philosophies that provide the basis for special education practice.

K2 Variations in beliefs, traditions, and values across cultures within society and the effect of the relationship among child, family, and schooling.

K3 Issues in definition and identification procedures for individuals with exceptional learning needs including individuals from culturally and/or linguistically diverse backgrounds.

K4 Issues, assurances, and due process rights related to assessment, eligibility, and placement within a continuum of services.

K5 Rights and responsibilities of parents, students, teachers and other professionals, and schools as they relate to individual learning needs.

*Skills:*

S1 Articulate personal philosophy of special education including its relationship to/with regular education.

S2 Conduct instructional and other professional activities consistent with the requirements of law, rules and regulations, and local district policies and procedures.

### CC: Common Core
### 2. Characteristics of Learners

*Knowledge:*

K1 Similarities and differences among the cognitive, physical, cultural, social, and emotional needs of individuals with and without exceptional learning needs.

*Skills:*

S1 Access information on various cognitive, communication, physical, cultural, social, and emotional conditions of individuals with exceptional learning needs.

**Skills:**

**Knowledge:**

K2  Differential characteristics of individuals with exceptionalities, including levels of severity and multiple exceptionalities.

K3  Characteristics of normal, delayed, and disordered communication patterns of individuals with exceptional learning needs.

K4  Effects an exceptional condition(s) may have on an individual's life.

K5  Characteristics and effects of the cultural and environmental milieu of the child and the family including cultural and linguistic diversity, socioeconomic level, abuse/neglect, and substance abuse.

K6  Effects of various medications on the educational, cognitive, physical, social, and emotional behavior of individuals with exceptionalities.

K7  Educational implications of characteristics of various exceptionalities.

---

**CC:  Common Core**
**3.    Assessment, Diagnosis, and Evaluation**

**Skills:**

S1  Collaborate with families and other professionals involved in the assessment of individuals with exceptional learning needs.

S2  Create and maintain records.

S3  Gather background information regarding academic, medical, and family history.

S4  Use various types of assessment procedures appropriately.

S5  Interpret information from formal and informal assessment instruments and procedures.

**Knowledge:**

K1  Basic terminology used in assessment.

K2  Ethical concerns related to assessment.

K3  Legal provisions, regulations, and guidelines regarding assessment of individuals.

K4  Typical procedures used for screening, prereferral, referral, and classification.

K5  Appropriate application and interpretation of scores, including grade score versus standard score, percentile ranks, age/grade equivalents, and stanines.

## Knowledge:

K6 Appropriate use and limitations of each type of assessment instrument.

K7 Incorporation of strategies that consider the influence of diversity on assessment, eligibility, programming, and placement of individuals with exceptional learning needs.

K8 The relationship between assessment and placement decisions.

K9 Methods for monitoring progress of individuals with exceptional learning needs.

## Skills:

S6 Report assessment results to individuals with exceptional learning needs, parents, administrators, and other professionals using appropriate communication skills.

S7 Use performance data and information from teachers, other professionals, individuals with exceptionalities, and parents to make or suggest appropriate modification in learning environments.

S8 Develop individualized assessment strategies for instruction.

S9 Use assessment information in making instructional decisions and planning individual programs that result in appropriate placement and intervention for all individuals with exceptional learning needs, including those from culturally and/or linguistically diverse backgrounds.

S10 Evaluate the results of instruction.

S11 Evaluate supports needed for integration into various program placements.

---

## CC: 4. Common Core Instructional Content and Practice

### Knowledge:

K1 Differing learning styles of individuals with exceptional learning needs and how to adapt teaching to these styles.

K2 Demands of various learning environments such as individualized instruction in general education classes.

K3 Curricula for the development of motor, cognitive, academic, social, language, affective, career, and functional life skills for individuals with exceptional learning needs.

K4 Instructional and remedial methods, techniques, and curriculum materials.

### Skills:

S1 Interpret and use assessment data for instruction.

S2 Develop and/or select instructional content, materials, resources, and strategies that respond to cultural, linguistic, and gender differences.

S3 Develop comprehensive, longitudinal individualized programs

S4 Choose and use appropriate technologies to accomplish instructional objectives and to integrate them appropriately into the instructional process.

*Knowledge:*

K5 Techniques for modifying instructional methods and materials.

K6 Life skills instruction relevant to independent, community, and personal living and employment.

K7 Cultural perspectives influencing the relationship among families, schools, and communities as related to effective instruction for individuals with exceptional learning needs.

K8 Impact of learners' attitudes, interests, values and academic and social abilities on intervention, instructional planning and career development.

*Skills:*

S5 Prepare appropriate lesson plans.

S6 Involve the individual and family in setting instructional goals and charting progress.

S7 Use task analysis.

S8 Select, adapt, and use instructional strategies and materials according to characteristics of the learner.

S9 Sequence, implement, and evaluate individual learning objectives.

S10 Integrate affective, social, and career/vocational skills with academic curricula.

S11 Use strategies for facilitating maintenance and generalization of skills across learning environments.

S12 Use instructional time properly.

S13 Teach individuals with exceptional learning needs to use thinking, problem-solving, and other cognitive strategies to meet their individual needs.

S14 Choose and implement instructional techniques and strategies that promote successful transitions for individuals with exceptional learning needs.

S15 Establish and maintain rapport with learners.

S16 Use verbal and nonverbal communication techniques.

S17 Conduct self-evaluation of instruction.

S18 Make immediate responsive adjustments to instructional strategies based on continual observations.

**CC: Common Core**
**5. Planning and Managing the Teaching and Learning Environment**

*Knowledge:*

K1 Basic classroom management theories, methods, and techniques for individuals with exceptional learning needs.

*Skills:*

S1 Create a safe, positive, and supportive learning environment in which diversities are valued.

*Knowledge:*

K2  Research-based best practices for effective management of teaching and learning.

K3  Ways in which technology can assist with planning and managing the teaching and learning environment.

*Skills:*

S2  Use strategies and techniques for facilitating the functional integration of individuals with exceptional learning needs in various settings.

S3  Prepare and organize materials to implement daily lesson plans.

S4  Incorporate evaluation, planning, and management procedures that match learner needs with the instructional environment.

S5  Design a learning environment that encourages active participation by learners in a variety of individual and group learning activities.

S6  Design, structure, and manage daily routines, effectively including transition time, for students, other staff, and the instructional setting.

S7  Direct the activities of a classroom volunteer or peer tutor.

S8  Direct, observe, evaluate, and provide feedback to paraeducator.

S9  Create an environment that encourages self-advocacy and increased independence.

S10 Maintain a safe environment where universal precautions are practiced.

---

**CC:   Common Core**
**6.    Managing Student Behavior and Social Interaction Skills**

---

*Knowledge:*

K1  Applicable laws, rules and regulations, and procedural safeguards regarding the planning and implementation of management of behaviors of individuals with exceptional learning needs.

K2  Ethical considerations inherent in behavior management.

K3  Teacher attitudes and behaviors that positively or negatively influence behavior of individuals with exceptional learning needs.

*Skills:*

S1  Demonstrate a variety of effective behavior management techniques appropriate to the needs of individuals with exceptional learning needs.

S2  Implement the least intensive intervention consistent with the needs of the individuals with exceptionalities.

S3  Modify the learning environment (schedule and physical arrangement) to manage inappropriate behaviors.

## Knowledge:

**K4** Social skills needed for educational and functional living and working environments and effective instruction in the development of social skills.

**K5** Strategies for crisis prevention/intervention.

**K6** Strategies for preparing individuals to live harmoniously and productively in a multiclass, multiethnic, multicultural, and multinational world.

## Skills:

**S4** Identify realistic expectations for personal and social behavior in various settings.

**S5** Integrate social skills into the curriculum.

**S6** Use effective teaching procedures in social skills instruction.

**S7** Demonstrate procedures to increase the individual's self-awareness, self-management, self-control, self-reliance, and self-esteem.

**S8** Prepare individuals with exceptional learning needs to exhibit self-enhancing behavior in response to societal attitudes and actions.

---

## CC: Common Core
## 7. Communication and Collaborative Partnerships

## Knowledge:

**K1** Factors that promote effective communication and collaboration with individuals with exceptional learning needs, parents, and school and community personnel in a culturally responsive program.

**K2** Typical concerns of parents of individuals with exceptional learning needs and appropriate strategies to help parents deal with these concerns.

**K3** Development of individual student programs working in collaboration with team members.

**K4** Roles of individuals with exceptionalities, parents, teachers, and other school and community personnel in planning an individualized program.

**K5** Ethical practices for confidential communication to others about individuals with exceptional learning needs.

## Skills:

**S1** Use collaborative strategies in working with individuals with exceptional learning needs, parents, and school and community personnel in various learning environments.

**S2** Communicate and consult with individuals, parents, teachers, and other school and community personnel.

**S3** Foster respectful and beneficial relationships between families and professionals.

**S4** Encourage and assist individuals with exceptional learning needs and families to become active participants in the educational team.

**S5** Plan and conduct collaborative conferences with individuals with exceptional learning needs and families or primary caregivers.

*Knowledge:*

K6 Roles and responsibilities of the paraeducator related to instruction, intervention and direct services.

K7 Family systems and the role of families in supporting child development and educational progress.

*Skills:*

S6 Collaborate with regular classroom teachers and other school and community personnel in integrating individuals with exceptional learning needs into various learning environments.

S7 Communicate with regular teachers, administrators, and other school personnel about characteristics and needs of individuals with specific exceptional learning needs.

---

## CC: Common Core
## 8. Professionalism and Ethical Practices

*Knowledge:*

K1 Personal cultural biases and differences that affect one's teaching.

K2 Importance of the teacher serving as a model for individuals with exceptional learning needs.

*Skills:*

S1 Demonstrate commitment to developing the highest educational and quality-of-life potential of individuals with exceptional learning needs.

S2 Demonstrate positive regard for the culture, religion, gender, and sexual orientation of individual students.

S3 Promote and maintain a high level of competence and integrity in the practice of the profession.

S4 Exercise objective professional judgment in the practice of the profession.

S5 Demonstrate proficiency in oral and written communication.

S6 Engage in professional activities that may benefit individuals with exceptional learning needs, their families, and/or colleagues.

S7 Comply with local, state, provincial, and federal monitoring and evaluation requirements.

S8 Use copyrighted educational materials in an ethical manner.

S9 Practice within the CEC Code of Ethics and other standards and policies of the profession.

# CEC Knowledge and Skills for All Beginning Special Education Teachers of Students with Disabilities in Individualized General Curriculums

| Individualized General Curriculum Referenced Standards | Area of Specialization Standard Included in This Item |
|---|---|
| **1. Foundations** | |
| **Knowledge:** | |
| 1 Current educational terminology and definitions of individuals with disabilities* including the identification criteria and labeling controversies, using professionally accepted classification systems, and current incidence and prevalence figures. | BD1K1;LD1K6;MR1K1;PH1K1 |
| 2 Evolution and major perspectives from medicine, psychology, behavior, and education on the definitions and etiologies of individuals with disabilities*. | BD1K3; LD1K2; MR1K2; MR6K1 |
| 3 Differing perceptions of deviance, including those from mental health, religion, legal-corrections, education, and social welfare. | BD1K2 |
| 4 The historical foundations, philosophies, theories and classic studies including the major contributors, and major legislation that undergird the growth and improvement of knowledge and practice in the field of special education*. | BD1K4; LD1K1; LD1K3; LD1K5; MR1K4; PH1 |
| 5 The legal system to assist individuals with disabilities*. | BD1K5 |
| 6 Continuum of placement and services, including alternative programs available for individuals with disabilities*. | MR1K3; BD6K2; DH1K6; PH1S2 |
| 7 Laws, regulations, and policies related to the provision of specialized health care in the educational setting. | PH1K4 |
| **Skills:** | |
| 1 Articulate the pros and cons of current issues and trends in the education of individuals with disabilities*. | BD1S1; LD1K4; LD1S2; MR1S1; PH1K3 |
| 2 Articulate the factors that influence the overrepresentation of culturally/linguistically diverse students in programs for individuals with disabilities*. | BD1S2; LD1S1; MR1S2 |
| 3 Delineate the principles of normalization versus the educational concept of "least restrictive environment" in designing educational programs for individuals with disabilities*. | BD1S3 |
| **2. Characteristics of Learners** | |
| **Knowledge:** | |
| 1 Physical development, physical disabilities, and health impairments as they relate to the development and behavior of individuals with disabilities*. | BD2K1; PH2K1 |
| 2 Effects of dysfunctional behavior on learning, and the differences between behavioral and emotional disorders and other disabling conditions. | BD2K3 |
| 3 Various etiologies and medical aspects of conditions affecting individuals with disabilities*. | LD2K1; LD2K2; LD2K4; MR2K1; MR2K2; PH2K2; PH2K3; PH2K4 |
| 4 Psychological and social-emotional characteristics of individuals with disabilities*. | BD2K2; LD2K3; LD2K5; MR2K4; MR2K5; PH2K1 |
| 5 Common etiologies and the impact of sensory disabilities on learning and experience. | DH2K4; DH2K6; DH2K8; DH2K9; DH2K10; VI2K1; VI2K3; VI3K5 |

*Implicit to all of the knowledge and skills standards in this section is the focus on individuals with disabilities whose education focuses on an individualized general curriculum.

1 Describe and define general developmental, academic, social, career, and functional characteristics of individuals with disabilities* as they relate to levels of support needed. — MR2S1

## 3. Assessment, Diagnosis, & Evaluation

**Knowledge:**

1 Specialized terminology used in the assessment of individuals with disabilities*. — BD3K3; LD3K1; MR3K2; PH3K1

2 Legal provisions, regulations, and guidelines regarding unbiased assessment and use of psychometric instruments and instructional assessment measures with individuals with disabilities*. — BD3K

3 Specialized policies regarding screening, referral, and placement procedures for individuals with disabilities*. — BD3K5; LD3K3; MR3K5; PH3K3

**Skills:**

1 Implement procedures for assessing and reporting both appropriate and problematic social behaviors of individuals with disabilities*. — BD3K2; BD3S1; BD3S2; MR3K3

2 Use exceptionality-specific assessment instruments with individuals with disabilities*. — BD3K1; BD3S3; LD3S1;MR3K3; MR3K4; MR3S1; PH3S4

3 Adapt and modify ecological inventories, portfolio assessments, functional assessments, and future-based assessments to accommodate the unique abilities and needs of individuals with disabilities*. — MR3K3; MR3S2; PH3S1

4 Develop and use a technology plan based on assistive technology assessment. — PH3S2

5 Assess reliable method(s) of response of individuals who lack typical communication and performance abilities. — PH3S3

## 4. Instructional Content & Practice

**Knowledge:**

1 Sources of specialized materials for individuals with disabilities*. — BD4K2; LD4K6; MR4K1

2 Impact of listening skills on the development of critical thinking, reading comprehension, and oral and written language. — LD4K1

3 Impact of language development on the academic and social skills of individuals with disabilities*. — LD4K2

4 Impact of disabilities on auditory skills. — LD4K3

5 Relationship between disabilities and reading instruction. — LD4K4

6 Impact of social skills on the lives of individuals with disabilities*. — LD4K5

7 Varied test-taking strategies. — LD4K7

8 Alternatives for teaching skills and strategies to individuals with learning disabilities who differ in degree and kind of disability. — LD4K8

9 Approaches to create positive learning environments for individuals with disabilities*. — MR4K3

**Skills:**

1 Use effective, research-based instructional strategies and practices to meet the needs of individuals with disabilities*. — BD4K1; BD4K3; LD4K8; LD4S1; LD4S11

2 Facilitate use of prevention and intervention strategies in educational settings. — BD4S1

3 Delineate and apply the goals, intervention strategies, and procedures related to psychodynamic, behavioral, biophysical, and ecological approaches to individuals with disabilities*. — BD4S2

*Implicit to all of the knowledge and skills standards in this section is the focus on individuals with disabilities whose education focuses on an individualized general curriculum.

| 4 | Plan, organize, and implement educational programs appropriate to the cognitive and affective needs of individuals with disabilities*. | BD4S4 |
| 5 | Evaluate, select, develop, and adopt curriculum materials and technology appropriate for individuals with disabilities*. | BD4S5; BD4S3 |
| 6 | Integrate academic instruction, affective education, and behavior management for individual learners and groups of learners. | BD4S9 |
| 7 | Evaluate strengths and limitations of alternative instructional strategies for individuals with disabilities*. | BD4S10 |
| 8 | Integrate student-initiated learning experiences into ongoing instruction. | BD4S11 |
| 9 | Use skills to enhance thinking processes. | LD4S3 |
| 10 | Use effective instructional strategies to assist individuals with disabilities* to detect and correct errors in oral and written language. | LD4S6, LD4S7, LD4S8 |
| 11 | Use appropriate instructional strategies to teach math skills and concepts according to the characteristics of the learner and patterns of error. | LD4S10 |
| 12 | Modify pace of instruction and use organization cues. | LD4S12 |
| 13 | Integrate appropriate teaching strategies and instructional approaches to provide effective instruction in academic and nonacademic areas for individuals with disabilities*. | LD4S13 |
| 14 | Utilize research-supported instructional strategies and practices, including the functional embedded skills approach, community-based instruction, task analysis, multisensory, and concrete/manipulative techniques. | MR4S1 |
| 15 | Design age-appropriate instruction based on the adaptive skills of learners. | MR4S4 |
| 16 | Integrate related services into the instructional settings of learners. | MR4S5 |
| 17 | Provide community referenced instruction. | MR4S6 |
| 18 | Assist students in the use of alternative and augmentative communication systems. | MR4S7 |
| 19 | Support the use of media, materials, alternative communication styles and resources required for learners whose disabilities interfere with communications. | DH4S3 |
| 20 | Interpret sensory, mobility, reflex, and perceptual information to create appropriate learning plans. | PH4S1 |
| 21 | Use appropriate adaptations and technology for all individuals with disabilities*. | PH4S2 |
| 22 | Adapt lessons that minimize the physical exertion of individuals with specialized health care needs. | PH4S3 |
| 23 | Design and implement an instructional program that addresses instruction in independent living skills, vocational skills, and career education for students with physical and health disabilities emphasizing positive self-concepts and realistic goals. | PH4S4 |
| 24 | Design and implement curriculum and instructional strategies for medical self-management procedures for students with specialized health care needs. | PH4S5 |
| 25 | Participate in the selection and implementation of augmentative or alternative communication devices and systems for use with students with physical and health disabilities. | PH4S6 |
| 26 | Use strategies for facilitating the maintenance and generalization of skills across learning environments. | VI4S4 |

## 5. Planning and Managing the Teaching and Learning Environment

**Knowledge:**

| 1 | Model career, vocational, and transition programs for individuals with disabilities*. | BD5K1; MR5K1 |
| 2 | Issues, resources, and techniques used to integrate students with disabilities into and out of special centers, psychiatric hospitals, and residential treatment centers. | BD5K2 |

*Implicit to all of the knowledge and skills standards in this section is the focus on individuals with disabilities whose education focuses on an individualized general curriculum.

3　Appropriate use of assistive devices to meet the needs of individuals with disabilities*. ... MR4K2; PH5K2

4　Common environmental and personal barriers that hinder accessibility and acceptance of individuals with disabilities*. ... PH5K4

**Skills:**

1　Monitor intragroup behavior changes across subjects and activities. ... BD5S1

2　Structure the educational environment to provide optimal learning opportunities for individuals with disabilities*. ... BD5S2; MR5S1; PH5K1

3　Teach individuals with disabilities* in a variety of educational settings. ... MR5S2

4　Design learning environments for individuals with disabilities* that provide feedback from peers and adults. ... LD6S1

5　Design learning environments that are multisensory and that facilitate active participation, self-advocacy, and independence of individuals with disabilities* in a variety of group and individual learning activities. ... V15S3; V15S4

6　Use local, community, state, and provincial resources to assist in programming with individuals who are likely to make progress in the general curriculum. ... PH5S1

7　Coordinate activities of related services personnel to maximize direct instruction time for individuals with disabilities*. ... PH5S2

## 6. Managing Student Behavior and Social Interaction Skills

**Knowledge:**

1　Rationale for selecting specific management techniques for individuals with disabilities*. ... BD6K1

2　Theories behind reinforcement techniques and their application to teaching individuals with disabilities*. ... BD6K3

3　Theories of behavior problems in individuals with disabilities*, including self-stimulation and self-abuse. ... MR6K1

4　Communication and social interaction alternatives for individuals who are nonspeaking. ... PH6K1

**Skills:**

1　Use a variety of nonaversive techniques for the purpose of controlling targeted behavior and maintaining attention of individuals with disabilities*. ... BD6S1

2　Develop and implement a systematic behavior management plan using observation, recording, charting, establishment of timelines, hierarchies of interventions, and schedules of reinforcement. ... BD6S2;BD6S4

3　Select target behaviors to be changed and identify the critical variables affecting the target behavior. ... BD6S3

4　Define and use skills in problem-solving and conflict resolution. ... BD6S5

5　Design, implement, and evaluate instructional programs that enhance an individual's social participation in family, school, and community activities. ... MR6S1

6　Establish a consistent classroom routine for individuals with disabilities*. ... BD4S6

7　Delineate and apply appropriate management procedures when presented with spontaneous management problems. ... BD4S7

8　Facilitate development and implementation of rules and appropriate consequences in the educational environment. ... BD4S8

## 7. Communication and Collaborative Partnerships

**Knowledge:**

1　Sources of unique services, networks, and organizations for individuals with disabilities*, including career, vocational, and transition support. ... BD7K1; LD7K1; MR7K1; PH7K1

*Implicit to all of the knowledge and skills standards in this section is the focus on individuals with disabilities whose education focuses on an individualized general curriculum.

2 Parent education programs and behavior management guides, including those commercially available, that address the management of severe behavioral problems and facilitate communication links applicable to individuals with disabilities*.  BD7K2

3 Collaborative and consultative roles of special education teachers in the integration of individuals with disabilities* into the general curriculum and classroom.  BD7K3

4 Types and importance of information generally available from family, school officials, legal system, community service agencies.  BD7K4

5 Roles and responsibilities of school-based medical and related services personnel, professional groups, and community organizations in identifying, assessing, and providing services to individuals with disabilities*.  BD7K5; PH7K2; PH7K3

**Skills:**

1 Use specific behavioral management and counseling techniques in managing students and providing training for their parents.  BD7S1

2 Assist students, in collaboration with parents and other professionals, in planning for transition to post-school settings with maximum opportunities for decision making and full participation in the community.  MR7S1

## 8. Professionalism and Ethical Practices

**Knowledge:**

1 Consumer and professional organizations, publications, and journals relevant to individuals with disabilities*.  BD8K1; LD8K1; MR8K1; PH8K2

2 Rights to privacy, confidentiality, and respect for differences among all persons interacting with individuals with disabilities*.  PH8K1

3 Types and transmission routes of infectious disease.  PH8K3

4 Maintain confidentiality of medical and academic records and respect for privacy of individuals with disabilities*.  PH8S2

**Skills:**

1 Participate in the activities of professional organizations relevant to individuals with disabilities*.  BD8S1; LD8S2; MR8S1; PH8S5

2 Articulate the teacher's ethical responsibility to nonidentified individuals who function similarly to individuals with disabilities*.  LD8S1

*Implicit to all of the knowledge and skills standards in this section is the focus on individuals with disabilities whose education focuses on an individualized general curriculum.

# CEC Knowledge and Skills for All Beginning Special Education Teachers of Students with Disabilities in Individualized Independence Curriculums

| Individualized Independence Curriculum Referenced Standards | Area of Specialization Standard Included in This Item |
|---|---|
| **1. Foundations** | |
| **Knowledge:** | |
| 1 Current educational terminology and definitions of individuals who would benefit most from a independence curriculum, including the identification criteria and labeling controversies, utilizing professional accepted classification systems and current incidence and prevalence figures. | BD1K1; DH1K1; MR1K1; PH1K1; VI1K3 |
| 2 Evolution and major perspectives from medicine, psychology, behavior, and education on the definitions and etiologies of individuals with disabilities*. | BD1K3; MR1K2 |
| 3 The historic foundations, classic studies including the major contributors, and major legislation that grounds the growth and improvement of knowledge and practice in the field of education of individuals with disabilities*. | BD1K4; MR1K4; PH1K2 |
| 4 Continuum of placement and services available for individuals with disabilities*. | DH1K6; MR1K3; PH1S1 |
| 5 Laws, regulations, and policies related to the provision of specialized health care in the educational setting. | PH1K4 |
| **Skills:** | |
| 1 Articulate the pros and cons of current issues and trends in the education of individuals with disabilities*. | BD1S1; MR1S1; PH1K3 |
| 2 Delineate the principles of normalization versus the educational concept of "least restrictive environment" in designing educational programs for individuals with disabilities*. | BD1S3 |
| **2. Characteristics of Learners** | |
| **Knowledge:** | |
| 1 Physical development, physical disabilities, sensory disabilities, and health impairments as they relate to the development and behavior of individuals who would benefit most from a functional independence curriculum. | BD2K1; DH2K6; DH2K8; DH2K9; DH2K10; PH2K1; VI2K1; VI3K5 |
| 2 The various etiologies and medical aspects of conditions affecting individuals with disabilities*. | DH2K4; MR2K1; MR2K2; PH2K3; |
| 3 Psychological and social-emotional characteristics of individuals with disabilities*. | BD2K2; MR2K4; MR2K5; PH2K1 |
| 4 Medical complications and implications for student support needs, including seizure management, tube feeding, catheterization, and cardiopulmonary resuscitation (CPR). | MR2K3 |
| **Skills:** | |
| 1 Describe and define general developmental, academic, social, career, and functional characteristics of individuals who would benefit most from a independent curriculum as they relate to levels of support needed. | MR2S1 |

*Implicit to all of the knowledge and skills standards in this section is the focus on individuals with disabilities whose education is in an individualized independence curriculum.

## 3. Assessment, Diagnosis, and Evaluation

### Knowledge:

1  Specialized terminology used in the assessment of individuals who would benefit most from a functional independence curriculum as they relate to levels of support needed.  BD3K3; MR3K2; PH3K1

2  Legal provisions, regulations, and guidelines regarding unbiased assessment and use of psychometric instruments and instructional assessment measures with individuals with disabilities* as they relate to levels of support needed.  BD3K4; MR3K1; PH3K2; BD3K1

3  Specialized policies regarding screening, referral, and placement procedures for individuals who would benefit most from a functional independence curriculum as they relate to levels of support needed.  BD3K5; MR3K5; PH3K3

### Skills:

1  Implement procedures for assessing and reporting both appropriate and problematic social behaviors of individuals with disabilities*.  BD3K2; BD3S1; BD3S2; MR3K3

2  Use exceptionality-specific assessment instruments with individuals with disabilities*.  BD3K1; BD3S3; DH3S3; MR3K3; MR3K4; MR3S1; PH3S4; VI3S2

3  Adapt and modify existing assessment tools and methods to accommodate the unique abilities and needs of individuals who would benefit most from a functional independence curriculum.  MR3S2; MR3K3; PH3S1; VI3S3

4  Develop and use a technology plan based on adaptive technology assessment.  PH3S2

5  Assess reliable method(s) of response of individuals who lack typical communication and performance abilities.  PH3S3

## 4. Instructional Content and Practice

### Knowledge:

1  The sources of specialized materials, equipment, and assistive technology for individuals with disabilities*.  BD4K2; LD4K6; MR4K1; PH4K2

2  The impact of language development on the academic and social skills of individuals with disabilities*.  LD4K2

3  The impact of disabilities on auditory skills of individuals with disabilities*.  LD4K3

4  The impact of social skills on the lives of individuals with disabilities*.  LD4K5

### Skills:

1  Facilitate use of prevention and intervention strategies in educational settings.  BD4S1

2  Use technology including assistive devices.  BD4S3

3  Use reinforcement systems to create effective learning environments.  BD4S4

4  Use student-initiated learning experiences and integrate them into ongoing instruction.  BD4S11

5  Use effective instructional strategies to assist individuals with disabilities* to detect and correct errors in oral and written language.  LD4S6;LD4S7

6  Choose appropriate methods and instructional strategies according to the characteristics of the learner.  LD4S8; LD4S9

7  Design and implement sensory stimulation programs.  MR4S2

8  Teach culturally responsive functional life skills.  MR4S3

9  Use research-supported instructional strategies and practices.  LD4S11

10  Design age-appropriate instruction based on the adaptive skills of learners.  MR4S4

11  Integrate related services into the instructional settings of learners.  MR4S5

*Implicit to all of the knowledge and skills standards in this section is the focus on individuals with disabilities whose education is in an individualized independence curriculum.

12 Provide community referenced and community based instruction. — MR4S6

13 Assist students in the use of alternative and augmentative communication systems. — MR4S7

14 Use appropriate physical management techniques, including positioning, handling, lifting, relaxation, and range — MR4S8

15 Facilitate learner's use of orthotic, prosthetic, and adaptive equipment. — MR4S9

16 Select and use media, materials, and resources required with learners whose disabilities interfere with communications. — DH4S3

17 Interpret sensory, mobility, reflex, and perceptual information to create appropriate learning plans. — PH4S1

18 Use appropriate adaptations and assistive technology. — PH4S2; CC4S2

19 Adapt lessons that minimize the physical exertion of individuals with specialized health care. — PH4S3

20 Design and implement instructional programs that address functional independence skills emphasizing positive self-concepts and realistic goals. — PH4S4

21 Design and implement strategies for medical self-management procedures. — PH4S5

22 Participate in the selection and implementation of augmentative or alternative communication devices and — PH4S6

## 5. Planning and Managing the Teaching and Learning Environment

**Knowledge:**

1 Model career, vocational, and transition programs for individuals with disabilities* who are most likely to make progress in a functional independence curriculum. — BD5K1; MR5K1

2 Issues, resources, and techniques used to integrate students in a functional independence curriculum into and out of alternative environments, including special centers, psychiatric hospitals, and residential treatment centers. — BD5K2

3 Appropriate use of assistive devices to meet the needs of individuals with disabilities*. — PH5K2

4 Specialized health care practices, first-aid techniques, and other medically relevant interventions necessary to maintain the health and safety of individuals with disabilities in a variety of educational settings. — PH5K3

5 Common environmental and personal barriers that hinder accessibility and acceptance of individuals with disabilities*. — PH5K4

**Skills:**

1 Monitor intragroup behavior changes across subjects and activities. — BD5S1

2 Structure the educational environment for optimal learning opportunities. — MR5S1; BD5S2

3 Teach individuals with disabilities who are in a functional independence curriculum in a variety of settings. — MR5S2

4 Design learning environments that provides feedback from peers and adults. — LD6S1

5 Design learning environments that are multisensory and that facilitate active participation, self-advocacy, and independence of individuals with disabilities* in a variety of group and individual learning activities. — VI5S3; VI5S4

6 Use local, community, state, and provincial resources to assist in programming. — PH5S1

7 Coordinate activities of related services personnel to maximize direct instruction time for individuals with disabilities* who are studying an individualized independence curriculum. — PH5S2

8 Use techniques of physical positioning and management of individuals with physical and health disabilities to ensure participation in academic and social environments. — PH5S3

9 Demonstrate appropriate body mechanics to ensure student and teacher safety in transfer, lifting, positioning, and seating. — PH5S4

*Implicit to all of the knowledge and skills standards in this section is the focus on individuals with disabilities whose education is in an individualized independence curriculum.

10  Use appropriate adaptive equipment such as wedges, seat inserts, and standers to facilitate positioning, mobility, communication, and learning for individuals with physical and health disabilities.  PH5S5

11  Use positioning techniques that decrease inappropriate tone and facilitate appropriate postural reactions to enhance participation.  PH5S6

## 6.  Managing Student Behavior and Social Interaction Skills

### Knowledge:

1  Rationale for selecting specific management techniques for individuals with disabilities*.  BD6K1

2  Continuum of alternative placements and programs available to individuals with disabilities*; state, provincial, and local services available; and the advantages and disadvantages of placement options and programs within the continuum of services.  BD6K2

3  Theories behind reinforcement techniques and their applications for teaching individuals with disabilities*.  BD6K3

4  Theories of behavior problems in individuals with disabilities*, including self-stimulation and self-abuse.  MR6K1

5  Impact of multiple disabilities on behavior and learning.  MR6K2

6  Communication and social interaction alternatives for individuals who are nonspeaking.  PH6K1

### Skills:

1  Use a variety of nonaversive techniques for the purpose of controlling targeted behavior and maintaining attention of individuals with disabilities*.  BD6S1

2  Develop and implement systematic behavior management plans for individuals with disabilities* using observation, recording, charting, timelines, intervention hierarchies, and schedules of reinforcement.  BD6S2; BD6S4

3  Select target behaviors to be changed and identify the critical variables affecting the target behavior.  BD6S3

4  Define and use skills in problem-solving and conflict resolution.  BD6S5

5  Design, implement, and evaluate instructional programs that enhance the individual's social participation in family, school, and community activities.  MR6S1

6  Develop and facilitate use of behavior crisis management plans.  BD4S7

7  Facilitate development and implementation of rules and appropriate consequences.  BD4S8

## 7.  Communication and Collaborative Partnerships

### Knowledge:

1  Sources of unique services, networks, and organizations for individuals with disabilities*, including career, vocational, and transition support.  BD7K1; LD7K1; MR7K1; PH7K1

2  Parent education programs and behavior management guides, including those commercially available, that address the management of severe behavioral problems and facilitate communication links applicable to individuals with disabilities*.  BD7K2

3  Collaborative and/or consultative roles of the special education teachers and paraeducators in the integration of individuals with disabilities* into general classrooms.  BD7K3

4  Types and importance of information generally available from family, school officials, legal system, community service agencies.  BD7K4

5  Roles and responsibilities of school-based medical and related services personnel, professional groups, and community organizations in identifying, assessing, and providing services to individuals with disabilities*.  BD7K5; PH7K2; PH7K3

*Implicit to all of the knowledge and skills standards in this section is the focus on individuals with disabilities whose education is in an individualized independence curriculum.

**Skills:**

1 Assist students, in collaboration with parents and other professionals, in planning for transition to adulthood including employment, community, and daily life, with maximum opportunities for decision making and full participation in the community. — MR7S1

2 Use strategies to work with chronically ill and terminally ill individuals and their families. — PH7S2

## 8. Professionalism and Ethical Practices

**Knowledge:**

1 Consumer and professional organizations, publications, and journals relevant to individuals with disabilities*. — BD8K1; LD8K1; MR8K1; PH8K2

2 Rights to privacy, confidentiality, and respect for differences among all persons interacting with individuals with disabilities*. — PH8K1

3 Types and transmission routes of infectious disease. — PH8K3

**Skills:**

1 Participate in the activities of professional organizations relevant to individuals with disabilities*. — BD8S1; LD8S2; MR8S1; PH8S5

2 Articulate the teacher's ethical responsibility to individuals who function similarly to individuals with disabilities* (e.g., individuals atrisk). — LD8S1

3 Seek information regarding protocols, procedural guidelines, and policies designed to assist individuals with disabilities* as they participate in school and community-based activities. — PH8S4

4 Maintain confidentiality of medical and academic records and respect for privacy of individuals with disabilities*. — PH8S2

*Implicit to all of the knowledge and skills standards in this section is the focus on individuals with disabilities whose education is in an individualized independence curriculum.

# CEC Knowledge and Skills for All Beginning Special Education Teachers of Students Who Are Deaf or Hard of Hearing

## KNOWLEDGE AND SKILLS STATEMENTS

### DH: Deaf or Hard of Hearing
### 1. Philosophical, Historical, and Legal Foundations of Special Education

*Knowledge:*

**K1** Models, theories, and philosophies that provide the basis for Current educational definitions of students with hearing loss, including identification criteria, labeling issues, and current incidence and prevalence figures.

**K2** Models, theories, and philosophies (e.g., bilingual-bicultural, total communication, oral/aural) that provide the basis for educational practice(s) for students who are deaf or hard of hearing, as consistent with program philosophy.

**K3** Variations in beliefs, traditions, and values across cultures and within society, and the effect of the relationships among children who are deaf or hard of hearing, their families, and schooling.

**K4** Issues in definition and identification procedures for individuals who are deaf or hard of hearing (e.g., cultural versus medical perspective).

**K5** Rights and responsibilities (e.g., Deaf Children's Bill of Rights) of parents, students, teachers, and schools as they relate to students who are deaf or hard of hearing.

**K6** The impact of various educational placement options (from the perspective of the needs of any given child who is deaf or hard of hearing and consistent with program philosophy) with regard to cultural identity and linguistic, academic, and social-emotional development.

*Skills:*

**S1** Apply understanding of theory, philosophy, and models of practice to the education of students who are deaf or hard of hearing.

**S2** Articulate pros and cons of current issues and trends in special education and the field of education of children who are deaf or hard of hearing.

**S3** Identify the major contributors to the growth and improvement of knowledge and practice in the field of education of children who are deaf or hard of hearing.

## DH: Deaf or Hard of Hearing
## 2. Characteristics of Learners

*Knowledge:*

K1 Communication features (visual, spatial, tactile, and/or auditory) salient to the learner who is deaf or hard of hearing that are necessary to enhance cognitive, emotional, and social development.

K2 Research in cognition related to children who are deaf or hard of hearing.

K3 Cultural dimensions that being deaf or hard of hearing may add to the life of a child.

K4 Various etiologies of hearing loss that can result in additional sensory, motor, and/or learning differences in students who are deaf or hard of hearing.

K5 Effects of families and/or primary caregivers on the overall development of the child who is deaf or hard of hearing.

K6 Effects that onset of hearing loss, age of identification, and provision of services have on the development of the child who is deaf or hard of hearing.

K7 Impact of early comprehensible communication on the development of the child who is deaf or hard of hearing.

K8 Recognition that being deaf or hard of hearing alone does not necessarily preclude normal academic development, cognitive development, or communication ability.

K9 The differences in quality and quantity of incidental language/learning experiences that children who are deaf or hard of hearing may experience.

K10 Effects of sensory input on the development of language and cognition of children who are deaf or hard of hearing.

*Skills:*

(None in addition to Common Core.)

## DH: Deaf or Hard of Hearing
### 3. Assessment, Diagnosis, and Evaluation

*Knowledge:*

K1 Specialized terminology used in the assessment of children who are deaf or hard of hearing.

K2 Components of an adequate evaluation for eligibility placement and program planning (e.g., interpreters, special tests) decisions for students who are deaf or hard of hearing.

K3 Legal provisions, regulations and guidelines regarding unbiased diagnostic assessment, and use of instructional assessment measures with students who are deaf or hard of hearing.

K4 Special policies regarding referral and placement procedures (e.g., *Federal Policy Guidance*, October 30, 1993) for students who are deaf or hard of hearing.

*Skills:*

S1 Administer appropriate assessment tools utilizing the natural/native/preferred language of the student who is deaf or hard of hearing.

S2 Gather and analyze communication samples from students who are deaf or hard of hearing, including nonverbal as well as linguistic acts.

S3 Use exceptionality-specific assessment instruments (e.g., SAT-HI, TERA-DHH, FSST) appropriate for students who are deaf or hard of hearing.

## DH: Deaf or Hard of Hearing
### 4. Instructional Content and Practice

*Knowledge:*

K1 Sources of specialized materials for students who are deaf or hard of hearing.

K2 Components of the nonlinguistic and linguistic communication that students who are deaf or hard of hearing use.

K3 The procedures and technologies required to educate students who are deaf or hard of hearing under one or more of the existing modes or philosophies (consistent with program philosophy).

K4 Information related to American Sign Language (ASL) and existing communication modes used by students who are deaf or hard of hearing.

*Skills:*

S1 Demonstrate proficiency in the language(s) the beginning teacher will use to instruct students who are deaf or hard of hearing.

S2 Demonstrate the basic characteristics of various existing communication modes used with students who are deaf or hard of hearing.

S3 Select, design, produce, and utilize media, materials, and resources required to educate students who are deaf or hard of hearing under one or more of the existing modes or philosophies (e.g., bilingual-bicultural, total communication, aural/oral).

## Knowledge:

**K5** Current theories of how languages (e.g., ASL and English) develop in both children who are hearing and those who are deaf or hard of hearing.

**K6** Subject matter and practices used in general education across content areas.

**K7** Ways to facilitate cognitive and communicative development in students who are deaf or hard of hearing (e.g., visual saliency) consistent with program philosophy.

**K8** Techniques of stimulation and utilization of residual hearing in students who are deaf or hard of hearing consistent with program philosophy.

**K9** Research-supported instructional strategies and practice for teaching students who are deaf or hard of hearing.

## Skills:

**S4** Infuse speech skills into academic areas as consistent with the mode or philosophy espoused and the ability of the student who is deaf or hard of hearing.

**S5** Modify the instructional process and classroom environment to meet the physical, cognitive, cultural, and communication needs of the child who is deaf or hard of hearing (e.g., teacher's style, acoustic environment, availability of support services, availability of appropriate technologies).

**S6** Facilitate independent communication behavior in children who are deaf or hard of hearing.

**S7** Apply first and second language teaching strategies (e.g., English through ASL or ESL) appropriate to the needs of the individual student who is deaf or hard of hearing and consistent with program philosophy.

**S8** Demonstrate the ability to modify incidental language experiences to fit the visual and other sensory needs of children who are deaf or hard of hearing.

**S9** Provide appropriate activities for students who are deaf or hard of hearing to promote literacy in English and/or ASL.

---

## DH: Deaf or Hard of Hearing
## 5. Planning and Managing the Teaching and Learning Environment

## Knowledge:

**K1** Deaf cultural factors that may influence classroom management of students who are deaf or hard of hearing.

**K2** Model programs, including career/vocational and transition, that have been effective for students with hearing losses.

## Skills:

**S1** Manage assistive/augmentative devices appropriate for students who are deaf or hard of hearing in learning environments.

**S2** Select, adapt, and implement classroom management strategies for students who are deaf or hard of hearing that reflect understanding of each child's cultural needs, including primarily visual Deaf culture where appropriate.

*Knowledge:*

*Skills:*

S3 Design a classroom environment that maximizes opportunities for visually oriented and/or auditory learning in students who are deaf or hard of hearing.

S4 Plan and implement instruction for students who are deaf or hard of hearing and who have multiple disabilities and special needs.

## DH: Deaf or Hard of Hearing
## 6. Managing Student Behavior and Social Interaction Skills

*Knowledge:*

K1 Processes for establishing ongoing interactions of students who are deaf or hard of hearing with peers and role models who are deaf or hard of hearing.

K2 Opportunities for interaction with communities of individuals who are deaf or hard of hearing on the local, state, and national levels.

*Skills:*

S1 Prepare students who are deaf or hard of hearing in the appropriate use of interpreters.

## DH: Deaf or Hard of Hearing
## 7. Communication and Collaborative Partnerships

*Knowledge:*

K1 Available resources to help parents of children who are deaf or hard of hearing deal with their concerns regarding educational options and communication modes/philosophies for their children.

K2 Roles and responsibilities of teachers and support personnel in educational practice for students who are deaf or hard of hearing (e.g., educational interpreters, tutors, and notetakers).

*Skills:*

S1 Teach students who are deaf or hard of hearing to use support personnel effectively (e.g., educational interpreters, tutors, and notetakers).

S2 Facilitate communication between the child who is deaf or hard of hearing and his or her family and/or other caregivers.

S3 Facilitate coordination of support personnel (e.g., interpreters) to meet the diverse communication needs of the student who is deaf or hard of hearing and his or her primary caregivers.

*Knowledge:*

K3  Effects of communication on the development of family relationships and strategies used to facilitate communication in families with children who are deaf or hard of hearing.

K4  Services provided by governmental and nongovernmental agencies or individuals in the ongoing management of children who are deaf or hard of hearing.

*Skills:*

---

## DH: Deaf or Hard of Hearing
## 8.   Professionalism and Ethical Practices

*Knowledge:*

K1  The process for acquiring the needed skills in modes/philosophies of education of students who are deaf or hard of hearing in which an individual was not prepared.

K2  Consumer and professional organizations, publications, and journals relevant to the field of education of students who are deaf or hard of hearing.

*Skills:*

S1  Actively seek interaction with adults in the Deaf community to maintain/improve ASL, English signs, or cues as consistent with program philosophy.

S2  Demonstrate the ability to interact with a variety of individuals who are deaf or hard of hearing on an adult-to-adult level.

S3  Provide families with the knowledge and skills to make appropriate choices needed to enhance the development and transition of their children who are deaf or hard of hearing.

S4  Participate in the activities of professional organizations relevant to the education of students who are deaf or hard of hearing.

# CEC Knowledge and Skills for All Beginning Special Education Teachers of Students in Early Childhood

## KNOWLEDGE AND SKILLS STATEMENTS

---

**EC: Early Childhood**
**1.  Philosophical, Historical, and Legal Foundations of Special Education**

---

*Knowledge:* *

*Skills:*

S1  Articulate the historical, philosophical, and legal basis of services for young children both with and without special needs.

S2  Identify ethical and policy issues related to educational, social, and medical services for young children and their families.

S3  Identify current trends and issues in early childhood education, early childhood special education and special education.

S4  Identify legislation that affects children, families, and programs for children.

---

**EC: Early Childhood**
**2.  Characteristics of Learners**

---

*Knowledge:* *

*Skills:*

S1  Apply theories of child development, both typical and atypical, and apply current research with emphasis on cognitive, motor, social-emotional, communication, adaptive, and aesthetic development in learning situations in family and community contexts.

---

* Indicators of the ECSE knowledge base beyond the common core are reflected in the ECSE skills statements. Refer to the conceptual base that appears in *Personnel Standards for Early Education and Early Intervention: Guidelines for Licensure in Early Childhood Special Education* (DEC, NAEYC, & ATE, 1995).

*Knowledge:*

*Skills:*

S2 Identify pre-, peri-, and postnatal development and factors such as biological and environmental conditions that affect children's development and learning.

S3 Identify specific disabilities, including the etiology, characteristics, and classification of common disabilities in young children, and describe specific implications for development and learning in the first years of life.

S4 Apply knowledge of cultural and linguistic diversity and the significance of sociocultural and political contexts for development and learning, and recognize that children are best understood in the contexts of family, culture, and society.

S5 Demonstrate understanding of (a) developmental consequences of stress and trauma, (b) protective factors and resilience, (c) the development of mental health, and (d) the importance of supportive relationships.

## EC: Early Childhood
## 3. Assessment, Diagnosis, and Evaluation

*Knowledge:* *

*Skills:*

S1 Assess children's cognitive, social-emotional, communication, motor, adaptive, and aesthetic development.

S2 Select and use a variety of informal and formal assessment instruments and procedures, including observational methods, to make decisions about children's learning and development.

S3 Select and administer assessment instruments and procedures based on the purpose of the assessment being conducted and in compliance with established criteria and standards.

* Indicators of the ECSE knowledge base beyond the common core are reflected in the ECSE skills statements. Refer to the conceptual base that appears in *Personnel Standards for Early Education and Early Intervention: Guidelines for Licensure in Early Childhood Special Education* (DEC, NAEYC, & ATE, 1995).

*Knowledge:*

*Skills:*

S4 Develop and use authentic, performance-based assessments of children's learning to assist in planning, communicate with children and parents, and engage children in self-assessment.

S5 Involve families as active participants in the assessment process.

S6 Participate and collaborate as a team member with other professionals in conducting family-centered assessments.

S7 Communicate assessment results and integrate assessment results from others as an active team participant in the development and implementation of the individualized education program (IEP) and individual family service plan (IFSP).S8 Monitor, summarize, and evaluate the acquisition of child and family outcomes as outlined on the IFSP or IEP.

S9 Select, adapt, and administer assessment instruments and procedures for specific sensory and motor disabilities.

S10 Communicate options for programs and services at the next level and assist the family in planning for transition.

S11 Implement culturally unbiased assessment instruments and procedures.

S12 Develop and use formative and summative program evaluation to ensure comprehensive quality of the total environment for children, families, and the community.

---

**EC: Early Childhood**
**4. Instructional Content and Practice**

*Knowledge:* *

*Skills:*

S1 Plan and implement developmentally and individually appropriate curricula and instructional practices based on knowledge of individual children, the family, the community, and curricula goals and content.

---

* Indicators of the ECSE knowledge base beyond the common core are reflected in the ECSE skills statements. Refer to the conceptual base that appears in *Personnel Standards for Early Education and Early Intervention: Guidelines for Licensure in Early Childhood Special Education* (DEC, NAEYC, & ATE, 1995).

*Knowledge:*

*Skills:*

S2   Develop an IFSP or IEP, incorporating both child and family outcomes in partnership with family members and other professionals.

S3   Incorporate information and strategies from multiple disciplines in the design of intervention strategies.

S4   Develop and select learning experiences and strategies that affirm and respect family, cultural, and societal diversity, including language differences.

S5   Plan for and link current developmental and learning experiences and teaching strategies with those of the next educational setting.

S6   Select intervention curricula and methods for children with specific disabilities including motor, sensory, health, communication, social-emotional, and cognitive disabilities.

S7   Implement developmentally and functionally appropriate individual and group activities using a variety of formats, including play, environmental routines, parent-mediated activities, small-group projects, cooperative learning, inquiry experiences, and systematic instruction.

S8   Develop and implement an integrated curriculum that focuses on children's needs and interests and takes into account culturally valued content and children's home experiences.

S9   Demonstrate appropriate use of technology, including adaptive and assistive technology.

S10  Employ pedagogically sound and legally defensible instructional practices.

S11  Implement nutrition and feeding strategies for children with special needs.

S12  Use appropriate health appraisal procedures and recommend referral and ongoing follow-up to appropriate community health and social services.

*Knowledge:*

*Skills:*

S13 Identify aspects of medical care for premature, low birth weight, and other medically fragile babies, including methods of care for young children dependent on technology and implications of medical conditions on child develop and family resources, concerns, and priorities.

S14 Recognize signs of emotional distress, child abuse, and neglect in young children and follow procedures for reporting known or suspected abuse or neglect to appropriate authorities.

## EC: Early Childhood
## 5. Planning and Managing the Teaching and Learning Environment

*Knowledge:* *

*Skills:*

S1 Make specific adaptations for the special needs of children who have unique talents, learning and developmental needs, or specific disabilities.

S2 Design plans that incorporate the use of technology, including adaptive and assistive technology.

S3 Select, develop, and evaluate developmentally and functionally appropriate materials, equipment, and environments.

S4 Establish and maintain physically and psychologically safe and healthy learning environments that promote development and learning.

S5 Provide a stimulus-rich indoor and outdoor environment that employs materials, media, and technology, including adaptive and assistive technology.

S6 Organize space, time, peers, materials, and adults to maximize child progress in group and home settings.

* Indicators of the ECSE knowledge base beyond the common core are reflected in the ECSE skills statements. Refer to the conceptual base that appears in *Personnel Standards for Early Education and Early Intervention: Guidelines for Licensure in Early Childhood Special Education* (DEC, NAEYC, & ATE, 1995).

**Knowledge:**

**Skills:**

S7  Implement basic health, nutrition, and safety management practices for young children, including specific procedures for infants and toddlers and procedures regarding childhood illness and communicable diseases.

**EC: Early Childhood**
**6. Managing Student Behavior and Social Interaction Skills**

**Knowledge:** *

**Skills:**

S1  Use individual and group guidance and problem-solving techniques to develop positive and supportive relationships with children; to encourage and teach positive social skills and interaction among children; to promote positive strategies of conflict resolution; and to develop personal self-control, self-motivation, and self-esteem.

S2  Select and implement methods of behavior support and management appropriate for young children with special needs, including a range of strategies from less directive, less structured methods (e.g., verbal support and modeling) to more directive, more structured methods (e.g., applied behavior analysis).

S3  Support and facilitate family and child interactions as primary contexts for learning and development.

**EC: Early Childhood**
**7. Communication and Collaborative Partnerships**

**Knowledge:** *

**Skills:**

S1  Establish and maintain positive, collaborative relationships with families.

* Indicators of the ECSE knowledge base beyond the common core are reflected in the ECSE skills statements. Refer to the conceptual base that appears in *Personnel Standards for Early Education and Early Intervention: Guidelines for Licensure in Early Childhood Special Education* (DEC, NAEYC, & ATE, 1995).

*Knowledge:*

*Skills:*

S2 Apply family systems theory and knowledge of the dynamics, roles, and relationships within families and communities.

S3 Demonstrate sensitivity to differences in family structures and social and cultural backgrounds.

S4 Assist families in identifying their resources, priorities, and concerns in relation to their child's development.

S5 Respect parents' choices and goals for children and communicate effectively with parents about curriculum and children's progress.

S6 Involve families in assessing and planning for their children, including children with special needs.

S7 Implement a range of family-oriented services based on the family's identified resources, priorities, and concerns.

S8 Implement family services consistent with due process safeguards.

S9 Evaluate services with families.

S10 Collaborate/consult with other professionals and with agencies in the larger community to support children's development, learning, and well-being.

S11 Apply models of team process in diverse service delivery settings.

S12 Employ various team membership roles.

S13 Identify functions of teams as determined by mandates and service delivery needs of children and families.

S14 Identify structures supporting interagency collaboration, including interagency agreements, referral, and consultation.

S15 Participate as a team member to identify dynamics of team roles, interaction, communication, team building, problem solving, and conflict resolution.

S16 Employ two-way communication skills.

*Knowledge:*

*Skills:*

S17 Evaluate and design processes and strategies that support transitions among hospital; home; and infant/toddler, preprimary, and primary programs.

S18 Administer, supervise, and consult with or instruct other adults.

S19 Employ adult learning principles in supervising and training other adults.

S20 Facilitate the identification of staff development needs and strategies for professional growth.

S21 Apply various models of consultation in diverse settings.

S22 Provide consultation and training in content areas specific to services for children and families and organization/development programs.

S23 Provide feedback and evaluate performance in collaboration with other adults.

---

## EC: Early Childhood
## 8. Professionalism and Ethical Practices

*Knowledge:* *

*Skills:*

S1 Adhere to the profession's code of ethical conduct.

S2 Serve as advocates on behalf of young children and their families, improved quality of programs and services for young children, and enhanced professional status and working conditions for early childhood special educators.

S3 Reflect upon one's own professional practice and develop, implement, and evaluate a professional development plan.

S4 Participate actively in professional organizations.

S5 Read and critically apply research and recommended practices.

---

*Indicators of the ECSE knowledge base beyond the common core are reflected in the ECSE skills statements. Refer to the conceptual base that appears in *Personnel Standards for Early Education and Early Intervention: Guidelines for Licensure in Early Childhood Special Education* (DEC, NAEYC, & ATE, 1995).

# CEC Knowledge and Skills for All Beginning Special Education Teachers of Students with Emotional and Behavioral Disorders

## KNOWLEDGE AND SKILLS STATEMENTS

---

**BD: Emotional/Behavioral Disorders**
**1. Philosophical, Historical, and Legal Foundations of Special Education**

*Knowledge:*

K1 Current educational terminology and definitions of students with emotional/behavioral disorders (E/BD), including the identification criteria and labeling controversies, utilizing professional accepted classification systems, and current incidence and prevalence figures.

K2 Differing perceptions of deviance, including those from mental health, religion, legal-corrections, education, and social welfare.

K3 Differences between etiology and diagnosis unique to a variety of theoretical approaches (biophysical, psychodynamic, behavioral, ecological) and their application for students with E/BD.

K4 The historical foundations and classic studies, including the major contributors, that undergird the growth and improvement of knowledge and practices in the field of E/BD.

K5 The legal system to assist students with E/BD.

*Skills:*

S1 Analyze and articulate current issues and trends in special education and the field of E/BD.

S2 Articulate the factors that influence the overrepresentation of culturally/linguistically diverse students in programs for individuals with E/BD.

S3 Delineate the principles of normalization versus the educational concept of "least restrictive environment" in designing educational programs for students with E/BD.

---

**BD: Emotional/Behavioral Disorders**
**2. Characteristics of Learners**

*Knowledge:*

K1 Physical development, physical disability, and health impairments as they relate to the development and behavior of students with E/BD.

*Skills:*

(None in addition to Common Core.)

*Knowledge:*

K2 Major social characteristics of individuals with E/BD.

K3 The effects of dysfunctional behavior on learning, and the differences between behavioral and emotional disorders and other disabling conditions.

## BD: Emotional/Behavioral Disorders
## 3. Assessment, Diagnosis, and Evaluation

*Knowledge:*

K1 Essential characteristics of valid behavior ratings scales.

K2 Processes involved in the diagnosis of students with E/BD, including academic and social behaviors in accordance with the current *Diagnostic and Statistical Manual of Mental Disorders* (DSM).

K3 Specialized terminology used in the assessment of E/BD.

K4 Legal provisions, regulations, and guidelines regarding unbiased assessment and use of psychometric instruments and instructional assessment measures with students with E/BD.

K5 Specialized policies regarding screening, referral, and placement procedures for students with E/BD.

*Skills:*

S1 Prepare accurate formal social assessment reports on students with E/BD based on behavioral-ecological information.

S2 Implement procedures for assessing both appropriate and problematic social behaviors of students with E/BD.

S3 Use exceptionality-specific assessment instruments appropriately for assessing students with E/BD.

## BD: Emotional/Behavioral Disorders
## 4. Instructional Content and Practice

*Knowledge:*

K1 Appropriate ways to apply research about students with E/BD in the classroom.

K2 Sources of specialized materials for students with E/BD.

*Skills:*

S1 Identify and use prevention and intervention strategies as early as appropriate for use with students with E/BD.

## Knowledge:

K3  Research-supported instructional strategies and practices for teaching students with E/BD.

## Skills:

S2  Delineate and apply the goals and intervention strategies and procedures related to a variety of theoretical approaches (including psychodynamic, behavioral, biophysical, and ecological) to students with E/BD.

S3  Use technology applicable to students with E/BD.

S4  Plan, organize, and implement individualized student programs appropriate to the cognitive and affective needs of the student with E/BD with special consideration to use of reinforcement systems and environmental conditions.

S5  Select, develop, adopt, and evaluate curriculum materials and technology applicable to students with E/BD.

S6  Establish a consistent classroom routine for students with E/BD.

S7  Delineate and apply appropriate management procedures when presented with spontaneous management problems applicable to students with E/BD.

S8  Establish classroom rules, as well as a means for enforcing these rules, that are applicable to students with E/BD.

S9  Integrate academic instruction, affective education, and behavior management for individual students and groups of students with E/BD.

S10 Evaluate strengths and limitations of the alternative instructional strategies designed for students with E/BD.

S11 Use student-initiated learning experiences and integrate them into ongoing instruction for students with E/BD.

## BD: Emotional/Behavioral Disorders
## 5. Planning and Managing the Teaching and Learning Environment

### Knowledge:

K1 Model programs, including career/vocational and transition, that have been effective for students with E/BD.

K2 Issues, resources, and techniques used to integrate students with E/BD into and out of alternative environments, including special centers, psychiatric hospitals, and residential treatment centers.

### Skills:

S1 Monitor intragroup behavior changes from subject to subject and activity to activity applicable to students with E/BD.

S2 Select a functional classroom design (e.g., functional seating, work area, storage) that is effective for students with E/BD.

## BD: Emotional/Behavioral Disorders
## 6. Managing Student Behavior and Social Interaction Skills

### Knowledge:

K1 Rationale for selecting specific management techniques for individuals with E/BD.

K2 Continuum of alternative placements and programs available to students with E/BD; state, provincial, and local services available; and the advantages and disadvantages of placement options and programs within the continuum of services.

K3 The theory behind reinforcement techniques and its application to teaching students with E/BD.

### Skills:

S1 Use a variety of nonaversive techniques (including voice modulation, facial expressions, planned ignoring, proximity control, and tension release) for the purpose of controlling targeted behavior and maintaining attention of students with E/BD.

S2 Develop and implement a systematic behavior management plan for students with E/BD using a variety of behavioral principles (including observation, recording, charting establishment of timelines, intervention technique hierarchies, and schedules of reinforcement).

S3 Select target behaviors to be changed and identify the critical variables affecting the target behavior (such as subsequent events and antecedent events).

S4 Designate certain pupil behaviors as either appropriate or inappropriate for a specific age group based on observation and social validation.

S5 Define and use skills in problem solving and conflict resolution.

## BD: Emotional/Behavioral Disorders
### 7. Communication and Collaborative Partnerships

**Knowledge:**

K1 Sources of unique services, networks, and organizations for students with E/BD.

K2 Parent education programs and behavior management guides, including those commercially available, that address the management of severe behavioral problems and facilitate communication links applicable to students with E/BD.

K3 Collaborative and/or consultative role of the special education teacher in the reintegration of students with E/BD (e.g., classroom/instructional modifications).

K4 Types and importance of information generally available from family, school officials, legal system, departments of social and health services, and mental health agencies.

K5 Role of professional groups and referral agencies in identifying, assessing, and providing services to children and youth with E/BD (e.g., mental health, corrections).

**Skills:**

S1 Use specific behavioral management and counseling techniques in managing students with E/BD and in providing training for their parents.

## BD: Emotional/Behavioral Disorders
### 8. Professionalism and Ethical Practices

**Knowledge:**

K1 Consumer and professional organizations, publications, and journals relevant to the field of E/BD.

**Skills:**

S1 Participate in the activities of professional organizations relevant to the field of E/BD.

# CEC Knowledge and Skills for All Beginning Special Education Teachers of Students with Gifts or Talents

## KNOWLEDGE AND SKILLS STATEMENTS

### GT: Gifted Education
### 1. Philosophical, Historical, and Legal Foundations of Special Education

*Knowledge:*

K1  The historical foundations and classic studies, including the major contributors, that undergird the growth of knowledge and practices in the field of gifted education.

K2  Current educational definitions of students with gifts and talents, including identification criteria, labeling issues, and current incidence and prevalence figures.

K3  Policies and issues at the national, state, and local levels that affect the education of students with gifts or talents.

K4  The impact of various educational placement options on individual students with gifts and talents with regard to cultural identity or economic class and physical, linguistic, academic and social-emotional development.

*Skills:*

S1  Articulate the pros and cons of current issues and trends in special education and the field of gifted education.

### GT: Gifted Education
### 2. Characteristics of Learners

*Knowledge:*

K1  Cognitive processing and affective characteristics of learners gifted in intellectual, creative, leadership, specific academic, visual/performing arts, and psychomotor domains.

K2  Enrichment and acceleration needs of gifted learners in required subject areas as compared with the needs of the general population of learners.

*Skills:*

(None in addition to Common Core.)

*Knowledge:*

K3 Cognitive and affective characteristics of "twice exceptional" special populations of gifted learners, such as culturally diverse, economically disadvantaged learners with learning, physical, or behavioral disabilities.

K4 The impact of multiple exceptionalities that result in additional sensory, motor, and/or learning needs.

K5 Effects of families and/or primary caregivers on the overall development of the child.

---

## GT: Gifted Education
## 3. Assessment, Diagnosis, and Evaluation

*Knowledge:*

K1 Specialized terminology used in the assessment of students with gifts and talents.

K2 Legal provisions, regulations, and guidelines regarding unbiased assessment and the use of instructional assessment measures with students with gifts and talents.

K3 Specialized policies regarding referral and placement procedures for students with gifts and talents.

*Skills:*

S1 Identify defensible (comprehensive, systematic, objective) and equitable procedures for identifying and placing learners with gifts and talents in appropriate programs and services.

S2 Use exceptionality-specific assessment instruments, both formal and informal, including learner interviews, for assessing students with gifts and talents.

S3 Evaluate learner products and portfolios appropriately.

---

## GT: Gifted Education
## 4. Instructional Content and Practice

*Knowledge:*

K1 Research-supported instructional strategies and practices (e.g., conceptual development, accelerated presentation pace, minimal drill and practice) for students with gifts or talents.

*Skills:*

S1 Design cognitively complex discussion questions, projects, and assignments that promote reflective, evaluative, nonentrenched thinking in students with intellectual or academic gifts or talents.

*Knowledge:*

K2   Sources of specialized materials for students with gifts or talents.

K3   Processes for designing opportunities for learners with gifts and talents to participate in community-based service learning for the development of ethics and social responsibility.

*Skills:*

S2   Select instructional model(s) appropriate to teaching topics, content area, or subject domain.

S3   Use instructional models; topic/domain instructional model matches commonly implemented in teaching gifted learners; and cognitive, creative, affective, and ethical taxonomies in order for higher levels to be addressed through instructional strategies.

---

**GT:   Gifted Education**
**5.   Planning and Managing the Teaching and Learning Environment**

*Knowledge:*

K1   Research-supported ability and achievement grouping practices and model programs, including career/vocational and transition (e.g., mentorships), that have been effective for students with gifts and talents.

K2   Curriculum and program planning models and research-supported accelerated practices that have been effective for students with gifts or talents.

*Skills:*

S1   Monitor and evaluate program activities for the purpose of continued program development or refinement.

---

**GT:   Gifted Education**
**6.   Managing Student Behavior and Social Interaction Skills**

*Knowledge:*

(None in addition to Common Core.)

*Skills:*

(None in addition to Common Core.)

## GT: Gifted Education
### 7. Communication and Collaborative Partnerships

*Knowledge:*

K1  Sources of unique services, networks, and organizations for students with gifts or talents.

K2  Principles of communication and collaboration and the role of the teacher within the various team models (e.g., multidisciplinary, interdisciplinary, transdisciplinary).

*Skills:*

(None in addition to Common Core.)

## GT: Gifted Education
### 8. Professionalism and Ethical Practices

*Knowledge:*

K1  Consumer and professional organizations, publications, and journals relevant to the field of gifted education.

*Skills:*

S1  Maintain knowledge of current research and literature in the field of special education and gifted education.

# CEC Knowledge and Skills for All Beginning Special Education Teachers of Students with Learning Disabilities

## KNOWLEDGE AND SKILLS STATEMENTS

**LD:   Learning Disabilities**
**1.   Philosophical, Historical, and Legal Foundations of Special Education**

### Knowledge:

K1   The historical foundations and classic studies, including the major contributors and advocacy organizations, that undergird the growth and improvement of knowledge and practices in the field of education of individuals who have learning disabilities.

K2   The evolution of the term *learning disability* as it relates to medicine, psychology, behavior, and education.

K3   Current and past philosophies and theories guiding the field of education of individuals who have learning disabilities.

K4   Future trends in the field of education of individuals who have learning disabilities.

K5   The influence of major legislation that affects individuals who have learning disabilities and the influence on practice.

K6   Current educational definitions of individuals with learning disabilities, including identification criteria, labeling issues, and current incidence and prevalence figures.

### Skills:

S1   Articulate the factors that influence overrepresentation of culturally and linguistically diverse individuals in programs for individuals with learning disabilities.

S2   Articulate the pros and cons of current issues and trends in special education and the field of learning disability.

## LD: Learning Disabilities
## 2. Characteristics of Learners

### Knowledge:

K1 The various etiologies of conditions affecting individuals with learning disabilities.

K2 The medical factors influencing individuals with learning disabilities, including medication, nutrition, genetics, and neurology.

K3 The psychological characteristics of individuals with learning disabilities, including intelligence, perception, memory, thinking skills, and language development.

K4 The relationship between individuals with learning disabilities and other associated conditions, including attention deficit disorder, attention deficit with hyperactivity, and dyslexia.

K5 The social/emotional aspects of individuals with learning disabilities, including social imperceptiveness, juvenile delinquency, and learned helplessness.

### Skills:

(None in addition to Common Core.)

## LD: Learning Disabilities
## 3. Assessment, Diagnosis, and Evaluation

### Knowledge:

K1 Specialized terminology used in the assessment of individuals who have learning disabilities.

K2 Legal provisions, regulations, and guidelines regarding unbiased assessment and use of instructional assessment measures with individuals who have learning disabilities.

K3 Specialized policies regarding referral and placement procedures for individuals who have learning disabilities.

### Skills:

S1 Choose and administer assessment instruments appropriately for individuals with learning disabilities.

# LD: Learning Disabilities
## 4. Instructional Content and Practice

### Knowledge:

K1 The impact of listening skills on the development of critical thinking, reading comprehension, and oral and written language.

K2 The impact of language development on the academic and social skills of individuals with learning disabilities.

K3 The impact of learning disabilities on auditory skills, including perception, memory, and comprehension.

K4 The relationship between learning disabilities and reading instruction, including reading purpose, rate, accuracy, fluency, and comprehension.

K5 The impact of social skills on the lives of individuals who have learning disabilities.

K6 Sources of specialized materials for individuals with learning disabilities.

K7 Various test-taking strategies used by individuals with learning disabilities.

K8 Alternatives for teaching skills and strategies to individuals with learning disabilities who differ in degree and kind of disability.

### Skills:

S1 Use effective instructional strategies for basic skills, including listening, reading, writing, reporting, and computing.

S2 Use effective instructional strategies for applying various study skills to academic areas.

S3 Use skills to enhance thinking processes.

S4 Use skills to enhance vocabulary development.

S5 Use appropriate reading methods for individuals who have learning disabilities.

S6 Use appropriate spelling methods and instructional strategies for individuals who have learning disabilities.

S7 Assist individuals who have learning disabilities in the prediction and detection of errors in oral and written language.

S8 Use appropriate handwriting methods and instructional strategies for individuals with learning disabilities.

S9 Use decision criteria for when to teach manuscript versus cursive writing for individuals with learning disabilities.

S10 Use appropriate math methods and instructional strategies including articulation, practice, immediate feedback, and review, for individuals who have learning disabilities and who show patterns of error.

S11 Use research-supported instructional strategies and practice for teaching individuals with learning disabilities.

S12 Modify speed of presentation and use organization cues.

S13 Integrate appropriate teaching strategies and instructional approaches to provide effective instruction in academic and nonacademic areas for individuals with learning disabilities.

## LD: Learning Disabilities
## 5.  Planning and Managing the Teaching and Learning Environment

*Knowledge:*

(None in addition to Common Core.)

*Skills:*

(None in addition to Common Core.)

## LD: Learning Disabilities
## 6.  Managing Student Behavior and Social Interaction Skills

*Knowledge:*

(None in addition to Common Core.)

*Skills:*

S1  Design a learning environment for individuals with learning disabilities that provides feedback from peers and adults.

## LD: Learning Disabilities
## 7.  Communication and Collaborative Partnerships

*Knowledge:*

K1  Sources of unique services, networks, and organizations for individuals with learning disabilities, including career/vocational support.

*Skills:*

(None in addition to Common Core.)

## LD: Learning Disabilities
## 8.  Professionalism and Ethical Practices

*Knowledge:*

K1  Consumer and professional organizations, publications, and journals relevant to the field of learning disabilities.

*Skills:*

S1  Articulate the learning disability teacher's ethical responsibility to nonidentified individuals who function similarly to individuals who have learning disabilities (e.g., at-risk individuals).

S2  Participate in the activities of professional organizations relevant to the field of learning disabilities.

# CEC Knowledge and Skills for All Beginning Special Education Teachers of Students with Mental Retardation and Developmental Disabilities

## KNOWLEDGE AND SKILLS STATEMENTS

---

### MR: Mental Retardation/Developmental Disabilities
### 1.  Philosophical, Historical, and Legal Foundations of Special Education

*Knowledge:*

K1  Current educational definitions of students/individuals with mental retardation/ developmental disabilities, including identification criteria, labeling issues, and current incidence and prevalence figures.

K2  Major perspectives on the definition/etiology of mental retardation/developmental disabilities.

K3  Continuum of placement and services available for students with mental retardation/ developmental disabilities.

K4  The historical foundations and classic studies, including the major contributors, that undergird the growth and improvement of knowledge and practices in the field of mental retardation/developmental disabilities.

*Skills:*

S1  Articulate the pros and cons of current issues and trends in special education and the field of mental retardation/developmental disabilities.

S2  Articulate the factors that influence the overrepresentation of culturally/linguistically diverse students in programs for individuals with mental retardation/developmental disabilities.

S3  Teach students with extensive disabilities, focusing on ability and similarities to children without disabilities.

---

### MR: Mental Retardation/Developmental Disabilities
### 2.  Characteristics of Learners

*Knowledge:*

K1  Causes and theories of intellectual disabilities and implications for prevention.

K2  Medical aspects of intellectual disabilities and their implications for learning.

*Skills:*

S1  Describe and define general developmental, academic, social, career, and functional characteristics of individuals with mental retardation/ developmental disabilities as they relate to levels of support needed.

*Knowledge:*

K3 Medical complications and implications for student support needs, including seizure management, tube feeding, catheterization, and CPR.

K4 Psychological characteristics of students with mental retardation/developmental disabilities, including cognition, perception, memory, and language development.

K5 The social-emotional aspects of mental retardation/developmental disabilities, including adaptive behavior, social competence, social isolation, and learned helplessness.

*Skills:*

---

**MR: Mental Retardation/Developmental Disabilities**
**3. Assessment, Diagnosis, and Evaluation**

*Knowledge:*

K1 Legal provisions, regulations, and guidelines regarding unbiased assessment and use of instructional assessment measures with students with mental retardation/ developmental disabilities.

K2 Specialized terminology used in the assessment of students with mental retardation/ developmental disabilities.

K3 Conditions and assessment instruments that ensure maximum performance for students with mental retardation/developmental disabilities.

K4 Adaptive behavior assessment.

K5 Specialized policies regarding referral and placement procedures for students with mental retardation/developmental disabilities.

*Skills:*

S1 Use exceptionality-specific assessment instruments such as adaptive skills assessments and developmental screening assessments.

S2 Adapt and modify existing assessment tools and methods to accommodate the unique abilities and needs of students with mental retardation/developmental disabilities, including ecological inventories, portfolio assessments, functional assessments, and future-based assessments.

# MR: Mental Retardation/Developmental Disabilities
## 4. Instructional Content and Practice

### Knowledge:

K1 Sources of specialized materials for students with mental retardation/developmental disabilities.

K2 Assistive devices for individuals with special needs.

K3 Approaches to create positive learning environments for individuals with special needs.

### Skills:

S1 Utilize research-supported instructional strategies and practices, including the functional embedded skills approach, community-based instruction, task analysis, multisensory, and concrete/manipulative techniques.

S2 Design and implement sensory stimulation programs for individuals with extensive needs.

S3 Teach culturally responsive functional life skills relevant to independence in the community, personal living, and employment, including accessing public transportation, cooking, shopping, laundry, functional reading, and sexuality.

S4 Design age appropriate instruction based on the adaptive skills of students with mental retardation/ developmental disabilities.

S5 Integrate selected related services into the instructional day of students with mental retardation/developmental disabilities.

S6 Provide instruction in community-based settings.

S7 Assist students in the use of alternative and augmentative communication systems.

S8 Use appropriate physical management techniques, including positioning, handling, lifting, relaxation, and range of motion.

S9 Use and maintain orthotic, prosthetic, and adaptive equipment effectively.

# MR: Mental Retardation/Developmental Disabilities
## 5. Planning and Managing the Teaching and Learning Environment

### Knowledge:

K1 Model programs, including career/vocational and transition, that have been effective for individuals with mental retardation/developmental disabilities.

### Skills:

S1 Structure the physical environment to provide optimal learning for students with mental retardation/developmental disabilities.

Skills:

S2  Demonstrate the ability to teach students with mental retardation/developmental disabilities in a variety of placement settings.

## MR: Mental Retardation/Developmental Disabilities
## 6.  Managing Student Behavior and Social Interaction Skills

Knowledge:

K1  Theories of behavior problems in individuals with mental retardation/developmental disabilities, including self-stimulation and self-abuse.

K2  Impact of multiple disabilities on behavior.

Skills:

S1  Design, implement, and evaluate instructional programs that enhance the student's social participation in family, school, and community activities.

## MR: Mental Retardation/Developmental Disabilities
## 7.  Communication and Collaborative Partnerships

Knowledge:

K1  Sources of unique services, networks, and organizations for students/individuals with mental retardation/developmental disabilities.

Skills:

S1  Assist students, with the support of parents and other professionals, in planning for transition to adulthood including employment and community and daily life, with maximum opportunities for full participation in the community and decision making.

## MR: Mental Retardation/Developmental Disabilities
## 8.  Professionalism and Ethical Practices

Knowledge:

K1  Consumer and professional organizations, publications, and journals relevant to the field of mental retardation/developmental disabilities.

Skills:

S1  Participate in the activities of professional organizations relevant to the field of mental retardation/developmental disabilities.

# CEC Knowledge and Skills for All Beginning Special Education Teachers of Students with Physical and Health Disabilities

## KNOWLEDGE AND SKILLS STATEMENTS

---

### PH: Physical and Health Disabilities
### 1. Philosophical, Historical, and Legal Foundations of Special Education

*Knowledge:*

K1 Current educational definitions of individuals with physical and health disabilities including identification criteria, labeling issues, and current incidence and prevalence figures.

K2 Historical foundations and classic studies, including the major contributors, that undergird the growth and improvement of knowledge and practices in the field of special education and related services for individuals with physical and health disabilities and their families.

K3 Contemporary issues in special education and related services for individuals with physical and health disabilities and their families.

K4 Laws, regulations, and policies related to the provision of specialized health care in the educational setting.

*Skills:*

S1 Articulate the service delivery for individuals with physical and health disabilities and its relation to contemporary educational placement and instructional content.

---

### PH: Physical and Health Disabilities
### 2. Characteristics of Learners

*Knowledge:*

K1 Implications of physical and health disabilities on psychosocial, educational, vocational, and leisure outcomes for individuals, families, and society.

*Skills:*

(None in addition to Common Core.)

*Skills:*

*Knowledge:*

K2 Generic medical terminology used to describe the impact of physical and health disabilities.

K3 Etiology and characteristics of physical and health disabilities across the life span.

K4 Secondary health care issues that accompany specific physical and health disabilities.

## PH: Physical and Health Disabilities
## 3. Assessment, Diagnosis, and Evaluation

*Knowledge:*

K1 Specialized terminology used in the assessment of individuals with physical and health disabilities.

K2 Legal provisions, regulations, and guidelines regarding unbiased assessment and use of instructional assessment measures of individuals with physical and health disabilities.

K3 Specialized policies regarding referral and placement procedures for students with physical and health disabilities.

*Skills:*

S1 Modify and adapt assessment procedures for use with individuals with physical and health disabilities.

S2 Develop and use a technology plan based on assitive technology assessment.

S3 Assess reliable method(s) of response of individuals who lack typical communication and performance abilities.

S4 Use results of specialized evaluations, such as oral motor, reflex, and movement, to make instructional decisions for individuals with physical and health disabilities.

## PH: Physical and Health Disabilities
## 4. Instructional Content and Practice

*Knowledge:*

K1 Research-supported instructional practices, strategies, and adaptations necessary to accommodate the physical and communication characteristics of students with physical and health disabilities.

*Skills:*

S1 Interpret sensory, mobility, reflex, and perceptual information to create appropriate learning plans for individuals with physical and health disabilities.

### Knowledge:

**K2** Sources of specialized materials, equipment, and assistive technology for students with physical and health disabilities.

### Skills:

**S2** Use appropriate adaptations and assistive technology such as switches, adapted keyboards, and alternative positioning to allow students with physical and health disabilities full participation and access to the core curriculum.

**S3** Adapt lessons that minimize the physical exertion of individuals with specialized health care needs.

**S4** Design and implement an instructional program that addresses instruction in independent living skills, vocational skills, and career education for students with physical and health disabilities, emphasizing positive self-concepts and realistic goals.

**S5** Design and implement curriculum and instructional strategies for medical self-management procedures by students with specialized health care needs.

**S6** Participate in the selection and implementation of augmentative or alternative communication devices and systems, including sign language, electronic devices, picture and symbol systems, and language boards, for use with students with physical and health disabilities.

---

## PH: Physical and Health Disabilities
## 5. Planning and Managing the Teaching and Learning Environment

### Knowledge:

**K1** School setting adaptations necessary to accommodate the needs and abilities of individuals with physical and health disabilities.

**K2** Appropriate use of assistive devices to meet the needs of individuals with physical and health disabilities.

**K3** Specialized health care practices, first aid techniques, and other medically relevant interventions necessary to maintain the health and safety of students in a variety of educational settings.

### Skills:

**S1** Use local, community, and state resources available to assist in programming for individuals with physical and health disabilities.

**S2** Coordinate activities of related services personnel to maximize direct instruction time for individuals with physical and health disabilities.

**S3** Use techniques of physical positioning and management of individuals with physical and health disabilities to ensure participation in academic and social environments.

*Knowledge:*

K4 Common environmental and personal barriers that hinder accessibility and acceptance of individuals with physical and health disabilities.

*Skills:*

S1 Use local, community, and state resources available to assist in programming for individuals with physical and health disabilities.

S2 Coordinate activities of related services personnel to maximize direct instruction time for individuals with physical and health disabilities.

S3 Use techniques of physical positioning and management of individuals with physical and health disabilities to ensure participation in academic and social environments.

S4 Demonstrate appropriate body mechanics to ensure student and teacher safety in transfer, lifting, positioning, and seating.

S5 Use appropriate adaptive equipment such as wedges, seat inserts, and standers to facilitate positioning, mobility, communication, and learning for individuals with physical and health disabilities.

S6 Use positioning techniques that decrease inappropriate tone and facilitate appropriate postural reactions to enhance participation.

S7 Practice recommended universal precautions to maintain healthy environments.

S8 Assist individuals to develop a sensitivity toward those who have communicable diseases.

S9 Monitor the effects of medication on individual performance.

S10 Integrate an individual's health care plan into daily programming.

---

**PH: Physical and Health Disabilities**
**6. Managing Student Behavior and Social Interaction Skills**

*Knowledge:*

K1 Communication and social interaction alternatives for individuals who are nonspeaking.

*Skills:*

(None in addition to Common Core.)

## PH: Physical and Health Disabilities
## 7. Communication and Collaborative Partnerships

*Knowledge:*

K1 Sources of unique services, networks, and organizations for individuals with physical and health disabilities.

K2 Roles and responsibilities of school-based medical and related services personnel (physical and occupational therapists, adapted physical education specialists, etc.).

K3 Roles and responsibilities of community-based medical and related services personnel (physicians, prosthetics, rehabilitation engineers, etc.).

*Skills:*

S1 Collaborate with service providers regarding acquisition, development, modification, and evaluation of assistive technology, procedures, and curricula to assist in meeting functional, social, educational, and technological needs of students with physical and health disabilities.

S2 Use strategies to work with chronically ill and terminally ill individuals and their families.

## PH: Physical and Health Disabilities
## 8. Professionalism and Ethical Practices

*Knowledge:*

K1 Rights to privacy, confidentiality, and respect for differences among all persons interacting with individuals with physical and health disabilities.

K2 Consumer and professional organizations, agencies, publications, and journals relevant to the field of physical and health disabilities.

K3 Types and transmission routes of infectious disease.

*Skills:*

S1 Participate in transdisciplinary team activities in providing integrated care for individuals with physical and health disabilities, particularly when students are transitioning from home, hospital, or rehabilitation facility to school.

S2 Maintain confidentiality of medical records and respect for privacy of individuals with physical and health disabilities.

S3 Practice appropriate universal precautions when interacting with individuals with physical and health disabilities.

S4 Seek information regarding protocols, procedural guidelines, and policies designed to assist individuals with physical and health disabilities as they participate in school and community-based activities.

S5 Participate in the activities of professional organizations relevant to the field of physical and health disabilities.

# CEC Knowledge and Skills for All Beginning Special Education Teachers of Students with Visual Impairments

## KNOWLEDGE AND SKILLS STATEMENTS

### VI: Visual Impairment
### 1. Philosophical, Historical, and Legal Foundations of Special Education

*Knowledge:*

K1 Federal entitlements (e.g., American Printing House for the Blind Quote Funds) that relate to the provision of specialized equipment and materials for learners with visual impairments.

K2 Historical foundations for education of children with visual impairments, including the array of service options.

K3 Current educational definitions of students with visual disabilities, including identification criteria, labeling issues, and current incidence and prevalence figures.

*Skills:*

S1 Articulate the pros and cons of current issues and trends in special education visual impairment.

### VI: Visual Impairment
### 2. Characteristics of Learners

*Knowledge:*

K1 Normal development of the human visual system.

K2 Basic terminology related to the structure and function of the human visual system.

K3 Basic terminology related to diseases and disorders of the human visual system.

K4 Development of secondary senses (hearing, touch, taste, smell) when the primary sense is impaired.

*Skills:*

(None in addition to Common Core.)

*Knowledge:*

K5 The effects of a visual impairment on early development (motor system, cognition, social/emotional interactions, self-help, language).

K6 The effects of a visual impairment on social behaviors and independence.

K7 The effects of a visual impairment on language and communication.

K8 The effects of a visual impairment on the individual's family and the reciprocal impact on the individual's self-esteem.

K9 Psychosocial aspects of a visual impairment.

K10 Effects of medications on the visual system.

K11 The impact of additional exceptionalities on students with visual impairments.

*Skills:*

---

# VI: Visual Impairment
## 3. Assessment, Diagnosis, and Evaluation

*Knowledge:*

K1 The impact of visual disorders on learning and experience.

K2 Specialized terminology used in assessing individuals with visual impairments, both as it relates to the visual system and in areas of importance.

K3 Ethical considerations and legal provisions, regulations, and guidelines (federal, state/provincial, and local) related to assessment of students with visual impairments (including the legal versus functional definitions of blindness and low vision).

K4 Specialized policies regarding referral and placement procedures for students with visual impairments.

*Skills:*

S1 Interpret eye reports and other vision-related diagnostic information.

S2 Use disability-specific assessment instruments appropriately (e.g., Blind Learning Aptitude Test, Tactile Test of Basic Concepts, Diagnostic Assessment Procedure).

S3 Adapt and use a variety of assessment procedures appropriately when evaluating individuals with visual impairments.

S4 Create and maintain disability-related records for students with visual impairments.

S5 Gather background information about academic, medical, and family history as it relates to the student's visual status for students with visual impairments.

K5 Procedures used for screening, prereferral, referral, and classifications of students with visual impairments, including vision screening methods, functional vision evaluation, and learning media assessment.

K6 Alternative assessment techniques for students who are blind or who have low vision.

K7 Appropriate interpretation and application of scores obtained as a result of assessing individuals with visual impairments.

K8 Relationships among assessment, IEP development, and placement as they affect vision-related services.

*Skills:*

S6 Develop individualized instructional strategies to enhance instruction for learners with visual impairments, including modifications of the environment, adaptations of materials, and disability-specific methodologies.

---

## VI: Visual Impairment
## 4. Instructional Content and Practice

*Knowledge:*

K1 Methods for the development of special auditory, tactual, and modified visual communication skills for students with visual impairments, including:
- Braille reading and writing.
- Handwriting for students with low vision and signature writing for students who are blind.
- Listening skills and compensatory auditory skills.
- Typing and keyboarding skills.
- The use of unique technology for individuals with visual impairments.
- The use of alternatives to nonverbal communication.

K2 Methods to acquire disability-unique academic skills, including:
- The use of an abacus.
- The use of a talking calculator.
- Tactile graphics (including maps, charts, tables, etc.).
- Adapted science equipment.

*Skills:*

S1 Interpret and use unique assessment data for instructional planning with students with visual impairments.

S2 Choose and use appropriate technologies to accomplish instructional objectives for students with visual impairments, and integrate the technologies appropriately into the instructional process.

S3 Sequence, implement, and evaluate individual disability-related learning objectives for students with visual impairments.

S4 Use strategies for facilitating the maintenance and generalization of disability-related skills across learning environments for students with visual impairments.

S5 Teach students who have visual impairments to use thinking, problem-solving, and other cognitive strategies to meet their individual learning needs.

## Knowledge:

K3 Methods for the development of basic concepts needed by young students who do not learn visually.

K4 Methods for the development of visual efficiency, including instruction in the use of print adaptations, optical devices, and non-optical devices.

K5 Methods to develop alternative reasoning and decision-making skills in students with visual impairments.

K6 Methods to develop alternative organization and study skills for students with visual impairments.

K7 Methods to prepare students with visual impairments for structured precane orientation and mobility assessment and instruction.

K8 Methods to develop tactual perceptual skills for students who are or will be primarily tactual learners.

K9 Methods to teach human sexuality to students who have visual impairments, using tactual models that are anatomically accurate.

K10 Methods to develop adapted physical and recreation skills for individuals who have visual impairments.

K11 Methods to develop social and daily living skills that are normally learned or reinforced by visual means.

K12 Strategies for developing career awareness in and providing vocational counseling for students with visual impairments.

K13 Strategies for promoting self-advocacy in individuals with visual impairments.

K14 Functional life skills instruction relevant to independent, community, and personal living and employment for individuals with visual impairments including:

- Methods for accessing printed public information.
- Methods for accessing public transportation.
- Methods for accessing community resources.
- Methods for acquiring practical skills (e.g., keeping personal records, time management, personal banking, emergency procedures).

## Skills:

*Knowledge:*

K15 Sources of specialized materials for students with visual impairments.

K16 Techniques for modifying instructional methods and materials for students with visual impairments, and assisting classroom teachers in implementing these modifications.

---

## VI: Visual Impairment
## 5. Planning and Managing the Teaching and Learning Environment

*Knowledge:*

K1 A variety of input and output enhancements to computer technology that address the specific access needs of students with visual impairments in a variety of environments.

K2 Model programs, including career-vocational and transition, that have been effective for students with visual impairments.

*Skills:*

S1 Prepare modified special materials (e.g., in Braille, enlarged, outlined, highlighted) for students who have visual impairments.

S2 Obtain and organize special materials to implement instructional goals for learners with visual impairments.

S3 Design learning environments that are multisensory and that encourage active participation by learners with visual impairments in a variety of group and individual learning activities.

S4 Create a learning environment that encourages self-advocacy and independence for students with visual impairments.

S5 Transcribe, proofread, and interline grade II Braille and Nemeth code Braille materials.

S6 Use Braillewriter, slate and stylus, and computer technology to produce Braille materials.

---

## VI: Visual Impairment
## 6. Managing Student Behavior and Social Interaction Skills

*Knowledge:*

K1 Teacher attitudes and behaviors that affect the behaviors of students with visual impairments.

*Skills:*

S1 Prepare students with progressive eye conditions to achieve a positive transition to alternative skills.

*Knowledge:*

*Skills:*

S2 Prepare students who have visual impairments to access information and services from the community at large.

S3 Prepare students who have visual impairments to respond to societal attitudes and actions with positive behavior, self-advocacy, and a sense of humor.

## VI: Visual Impairment
## 7. Communication and Collaborative Partnerships

*Knowledge:*

K1 Strategies for assisting parents and other professionals in planning appropriate transitions for students who have visual impairments.

K2 Sources of unique services, networks, and organizations for students with visual impairments.

K3 Roles of paraprofessionals who work directly with students who have visual impairments (e.g., sighted readers, transcribers, aides) or who provide special materials to them.

K4 Need for role models who have visual impairments, and who are successful.

*Skills:*

S1 Help parents and other professionals to understand the impact of a visual impairment on learning and experience.

S2 Report disability-related results of evaluations to students who have visual impairments, their parents and administrators and other professionals in clear, concise, "laymen's" terms.

S3 Manage and direct the activities of paraprofessionals or peer tutors who work with students who have visual impairments.

## VI: Visual Impairment
## 8. Professionalism and Ethical Practices

*Knowledge:*

K1 Consumer and professional organizations, publications, and journals relevant to the field of visual impairment.

*Skills:*

S1 Belong to and participate in the activities of professional organizations in the field of visual impairment.

# CEC Knowledge and Skills for
# Beginning Special Educational Diagnosticians*

## KNOWLEDGE AND SKILLS STATEMENTS

### ED: Educational Diagnostician
### 1. Philosophical, Historical, and Legal Foundations of Special Education

*Knowledge:*

K1 Various philosophies of assessment.

K2 Legal issues and regulations related to the assessment of an educational disability.

*Skills:*

S1 (None in addition to the required knowledge and skills for all beginning special education teachers.)

### ED: Educational Diagnostician
### 2. Characteristics of Learners

*Knowledge:*

K1 Variability of individual ability within categories of disability.

K2 Disproportionate representation and stig-matization in special education of populations that are culturally and linguistically diverse.

K3 Influences of diversity on assessment results.

*Skills:*

S1 (None in addition to the required knowledge and skills for all beginning special education teachers.)

### ED: Educational Diagnostician
### 3. Assessment, Diagnosis, and Evaluation

*Knowledge:*

K1 Standards for test reliability.

*Skills:*

S1 Select and utilize assessment materials based on technical quality.

* These standards assume that the entry-level educational diagnostician has previous mastery of the CEC Common Core of Knowledge and Skills Essential for All Beginning Special Education Teachers and the required CEC knowledge and skills in at least one area of special education teaching specialization.

*Knowledge:*

K2 Standards for test validity.

K3 Procedures used in standardizing assessment instruments.

K4 Possible sources of test error.

K5 Use of standard error of measure in the field of measurement.

K6 Uses and limitations of various types of assessment information.

K7 Vocational and career assessment.

K8 Motor skills assessment.

*Skills:*

S2 Collect complete and thorough assessment data.

S3 Accurate scoring of assessment instruments.

S4 Select or modify assessment procedures to ensure nonbiased results.

S5 Select or modify appropriate assessment procedures and instruments.

S6 Use a variety of observation techniques.

S7 Assess basic academic skills.

S8 Assess language skills.

S9 Assess adaptive behavior.

S10 Assess behavior.

S11 Assess perceptual skills.

S12 Determine a student's needs in various curricular areas and make intervention, instructional, and transition planning recommendations based on assessment results.

S13 Make eligibility recommendations based on assessment results.

## ED: Educational Diagnostician
## 4. Instructional Content and Practice

*Knowledge:*

K1 (None in addition to the required knowledge and skills for all beginning special education teachers.)

*Skills:*

S1 (None in addition to the required knowledge and skills for all beginning special education teachers.)

## ED: Educational Diagnostician
## 5. Planning and Managing the Teaching and Learning Environment

*Knowledge:*

K1 (None in addition to the required knowledge and skills for all beginning special education teachers.)

*Skills:*

S1 (None in addition to the required knowledge and skills for all beginning special education teachers.)

**ED: Educational Diagnostician**
**6. Managing Student Behavior and Social Interaction Skills**

*Knowledge:*

K1 (None in addition to the required knowledge and skills for all beginning special education teachers.)

*Skills:*

S1 (None in addition to the required knowledge and skills for all beginning special education teachers.)

**ED: Educational Diagnostician**
**7. Communication and Collaborative Partnerships**

*Knowledge:*

K1 (None in addition to the required knowledge and skills for all beginning special education teachers.)

*Skills:*

S1 *Skills:*

S1 Prepare assessment reports.

S2 Teach others informal and observational techniques of data collection.

S3 Effectively communicate the assessment purpose, methods, findings, and implications to parents and professionals.

S4 Keep accurate and detailed records of assessment and related proceedings.

**ED: Educational Diagnostician**
**8. Professionalism and Ethical Practices**

*Knowledge:*

K1 Qualifications necessary to administer and interpret tests.

K2 Scope and role of an educational diagnostician.

*Skills:*

S1 (None in addition to the required knowledge and skills for all beginning special education teachers.)

# CEC Knowledge and Skills for
# Beginning Special Education Administrators*

## KNOWLEDGE AND SKILLS STATEMENTS

## SA: Special Education Administrator
## 1. Philosophical, Historical, and Legal Foundations of Special Education

### Knowledge:

K1 National/federal, state, provincial, and local education reforms and their requirements for both general and special education.

K2 Historical and evolving special education policies, including laws, regulations, and procedures that impact the lives of individuals with exceptionalities and their families from birth through adulthood.

K3 Systems and systems theory including political and economic issues that affect policy development within state and local education agencies and across other human service systems.

K4 Models, theories, and philosophies that provide the basis for general educational systems.

### Skills:

S1 Develop an inclusive vision for meeting the needs of individuals with exceptionalities and communicate it to the various publics and constituencies throughout the school, community, and state/province.

S2 Interpret and communicate to various constituencies the evolving case law and federal, state, and local policies and practices pertaining to individuals with exceptionalities.

S3 Influence the development and implementation of appropriate policies for individuals with exceptionalities and their families.

## SA: Special Education Administrator
## 2. Characteristics of Learners

### Knowledge:

K1 Theories of child and adolescent development and principles of learning and how they relate to individuals with exceptionalities.

K2 Differential characteristics of individuals with exceptionalities and implications for the development of programs and services.

### Skills:

S1 Develop and implement programs that respond to individual and family characteristics, cultures, and needs within a continuum of services.

---

\* These standards assume that the entry-level special education administrator has previous mastery of the CEC Common Core of Knowledge and Skills Essential for All Beginning Special Education Teachers and the required CEC knowledge and skills in at least one area of special education teaching specialization.

## SA: Special Education Administrator
## 3. Assessment, Diagnosis, and Evaluation

### Knowledge:

K1 Current legal and policy issues surrounding assessment, program evaluation, and accountability related to students with exceptionalities.

K2 Principles of assessment of individuals with exceptionalities, including the use of valid and reliable instruments and procedures and their appropriate uses for eligibility determination, the development of individualized education programs, and monitoring student progress.

K3 Characteristics, appropriate use, and interpretation of various types of instructional assessments, including norm-referenced, performance-based, portfolio, and other authentic assessments.

### Skills:

S1 Advocate for the participation of individuals with exceptionalities in the local, provincial, and state accountability systems.

S2 Implement an assessment program for individuals with exceptionalities that is linked to the general system assessments, provides appropriate accommodations and/or valid alternative assessments, and documents learner progress toward educational goals.

S3 Understand and interpret information about individual students and their families within diverse cultural and linguistic contexts.

---

## SA: Special Education Administrator
## 4. Instructional Content and Practice

### Knowledge:

K1 General education curriculum theory, instruction, and how special education services support access to the general education curriculum for all students.

K2 General education curriculum theory and models and implications for diverse learners.

### Skills:

S1 Ensure that postschool outcomes for individuals with exceptionalities are addressed in the general system standards and curriculum.

S2 Develop and implement strategies to support teachers of individuals with exceptionalities and other service providers through professional development programs and constructive evaluation procedures that are designed to improve instructional content and practices.

S3 Develop and implement a plan that provides a wide array of instructional and assistive technologies for learning environments.

*Knowledge:*

*Skills:*

S4 Assist in the development and implementation of a range of curriculum and instructional options at the system and building levels that provide appropriate experiences for all students, including individuals with exceptionalities.

S5 Develop collaborative general and special education programs and other innovative approaches to ensure that individuals with exceptionalities have access to and appropriately participate in the general education curriculum and instructional programs.

S6 Support site-based decision-making processes and ensure that decisions and management procedures provide appropriate services to individuals with exceptionalities.

## SA: Special Education Administrator
## 5. Planning and Managing the Teaching and Learning Environment

*Knowledge:*

K1 Research related to educational innovation and change and its application to implementing new policies and practices.

K2 A wide array of curriculum and instructional programs designed for individuals with exceptionalities to promote the development of critical knowledge and skills in areas of academics, functional living, career/employment, social and emotional well-being, and physical health and wellness.

K3 Federal, state/provincial, and local fiscal policies related to education and other social and health agencies.

K4 Transition policies, programs, and practices designed to facilitate the seamless movement of students from early childhood into K–12 environments and from school to postsecondary settings.

K5 Human resources management, including recruitment, personnel assistance and development, and evaluation.

*Skills:*

S1 Develop and implement ongoing evaluations of district special education programs and practices.

S2 Develop and implement strategic plans and intra- and interagency agreements that create system-linked programs with shared responsibility for individuals with exceptionalities.

S3 Develop and implement flexible service delivery programs based on effective practices that address the range of individuals with exceptionalities and include prevention strategies.

S4 Develop and implement professional development programs for individuals, school sites, and district personnel that reflect teacher development research and strategies and include use of technology.

S5 Develop district budgets and procure funding from federal, state/provincial, and local sources to ensure the efficient and effective allocation of resources.

*Knowledge:*

K6 Regular and ongoing evaluation of individual student, site, and district services related to learning outcomes for all students.

K7 Program evaluation models, processes, and accountability systems.

*Skills:*

S6 Develop and implement strategies that promote seamless transitions of individuals with exceptionalities across educational and other programs from birth through adulthood.

S7 Use a variety of technologies to enhance efficient management of resources and programs.

---

## SA: Special Education Administrator
## 6. Managing Student Behavior and Social Interaction Skills

*Knowledge:*

K1 Federal, state/provincial, and district policies and procedures governing the discipline of all students and the implications for individuals with exceptionalities.

K2 Knowledge of legal and ethical issues surrounding use of various forms of behavior management procedures with individuals with exceptionalities.

*Skills:*

S1 Develop and implement a district discipline policy and procedures for individuals with exceptionalities, including procedures for individualized education program (IEP) development.

S2 Support program sites in implementing a range of strategies that promote positive behavior, including crisis intervention and family support and involvement.

---

## SA: Special Education Administrator
## 7. Communication and Collaborative Partnerships

*Knowledge:*

K1 Family systems and the role of families in supporting child development and educational progress.

K2 Approaches for involving parents, family, and community members in educational planning, implementation, and evaluation.

K3 The role of parent and advocacy organizations as they support individuals with exceptionalities and their families.

*Skills:*

S1 Implement a variety of management and administrative procedures to ensure clear communication among administrators and between administrators and instructional staff and related service personnel.

S2 Develop parent/family education and other support programs.

*Knowledge:*

*Skills:*

S3 Plan, communicate, and negotiate student and family needs and programs within the state/province, local district—including local schools—and other public and private service agencies.

S4 Develop and support communication and collaboration with educational and other public and private agency administrators at all levels.

S5 Collaborate and engage in shared decision making with building and agency administrators to support appropriate programs for individuals with exceptionalities.

S6 Develop and provide effective and ongoing communication with parents and families of individuals with exceptionalities.

S7 Use effective consultation and collaboration techniques in administrative and intervention and instructional settings.

---

## SA: Special Education Administrator
## 8. Professionalism and Ethical Practices

*Knowledge:*

K1 Racial, ethnic, gender, disability, class, and life-style issues that define the culture of the local community or state/province and their impact on educational expectations and programming for all students.

*Skills:*

S1 Serve as the advocate for individuals with exceptionalities and their families at the district level.

S2 Respect and support students' self-advocacy efforts.

S3 Communicate and demonstrate a high standard of ethical practice.

S4 Make decisions concerning individuals with exceptionalities based on open communication, trust, mutual respect, and dignity.

# CEC Knowledge and Skills for Beginning Transition Specialists*

## KNOWLEDGE AND SKILLS STATEMENTS

### TS: Transition Specialists
### 1. Philosophical, Historical, and Legal Foundations of Special Education

*Knowledge:*

K1  Theoretical and applied models of transition.

K2  Transition-related legislation in fields of special and vocational education, rehabilitation, labor, and civil rights.

K3  Roles of federal, state, provincial, and local legislation and implications for providing transition services at the local levels.

K4  History of national transition initiatives.

K5  Research on student outcomes and effective transition practices.

*Skills:*

S1  (None in addition to the required knowledge and skills for all beginning special education teachers.)

### TS: Transition Specialists
### 2. Characteristics of Learners

*Knowledge:*

K1  Implications of student characteristics with respect to postschool outcomes, environments, and support needs.

K2  School and postschool services available to specific populations of individuals with exceptional learning needs.

*Skills:*

S1  (None in addition to the required knowledge and skills for all beginning special education teachers.)

---

* These standards assume that the entry-level transition specialist has previous mastery of the CEC Common Core of Knowledge and Skills Essential for All Beginning Special Education Teachers and the required CEC knowledge and skills in at least one area of special education teaching specialization.

## TS: Transition Specialists
## 3.  Assessment, Diagnosis, and Evaluation

### Knowledge:

K1  Formal and informal career and vocational assessment approaches.

K2  Formal and informal approaches for identifying students' interests and preferences related to postschool goals and educational experiences.

### Skills:

S1  Match skills and interests of the student to skills and demands required by vocational or employment settings, community residential situation, and other community participation options.

S2  Interpret results of career and vocational assessment for individuals, families, and professionals.

S3  In collaboration with individuals with exceptional learning needs, families, and agencies, design, implement, and use program evaluation procedures to assess and improve the effectiveness of transition education and services, including evaluation of students' postschool outcomes.

S4  Use a variety of formal and informal career, transition, and vocational assessment procedures.


## TS: Transition Specialists
## 4.  Instructional Content and Practice

### Knowledge:

K1  Job seeking and job retention skills identified by employers as essential for successful employment.

K2  Vocational education methods, models, and curricula.

K3  Range of postschool options within specific outcome areas.

K4  Transition planning strategies that facilitate information collection and input from appropriate participants.

### Skills:

S1  Identify a variety of outcomes and instructional options specific to the community for each postschool outcome area.

S2  Assist teachers to identify, in conjunction with the student, appropriate educational program planning team members.

S3  Evaluate students' educational program with respect to measurable postschool goals and alignment of those goals with instructional activities.

S4  Monitor student, family, and agency participation in transition planning and implementation.

S5  Demonstrate procedures to ensure the inclusion of specific transition-related goals in the educational program plan.

**Knowledge:**

**Skills:**

S6 Evaluate and modify transition goals on an ongoing basis.

S7 Use interests and preferences of the individual with exceptional learning needs to develop postschool goals and educational objectives.

---

**TS: Transition Specialists**
**5. Planning and Managing the Teaching and Learning Environment**

**Knowledge:**

K1 Methods for providing work-based and other community-based education for individuals with exceptional learning needs.

K2 Methods for linking appropriate academic content to transition-related goals.

**Skills:**

S1 Identify and facilitate appropriate modifications within work, residential, vocational training, and other community environments.

S2 Assess and develop natural support systems to facilitate transition to specific postschool environments.

S3 Develop residential, work-based, and other community-based educational programs for individuals with exceptional learning needs.

---

**TS: Transition Specialists**
**6. Managing Student Behavior and Social Interaction Skills**

**Knowledge:**

K1 (None in addition to the required knowledge and skills for all beginning special education teachers.)

**Skills:**

S1 Demonstrate procedures for student involvement in the postschool transition process.

---

**TS: Transition Specialists**
**7. Communication and Collaborative Partnerships**

**Knowledge:**

K1 Methods and strategies for increasing families' knowledge and skills about transition-related issues and topics, including transition-focused educational program development.

**Skills:**

S1 Provide information to families about transition-related education and services, and postschool options in specific outcome areas.

*Knowledge:*

K2  Procedures and requirements for referring students to community service agencies.

K3  Methods to increase collaborative transition service delivery through interagency agreements and collaborative funding.

K4  Strategies for involving individuals with exceptional learning needs in all levels of collaborative transition program planning and evaluation.

*Skills:*

S2  Systematically identify family service needs related to transition outcomes and assist families to connect with support networks.

S3  Involve individuals with exceptional learning needs, families, and community agencies in establishing transition-related policy.

S4  Assess and use student support systems to facilitate the postschool transition of individuals with exceptional learning needs.

S5  Provide transition-focused technical assistance and professional development in collaboration with family members for educators, community agency personnel, and other relevant transition stakeholders.

S6  Collaborate with and participate in transition-focused interagency coordinating bodies.

S7  Develop coordinated interagency strategies to collect, share, and use student assessment data, with appropriate input and authorization of students and families.

S8  Use strategies for resolving differences that may arise in the implementation of interagency agreements or the provision of transition services for individuals with exceptional learning needs.

S9  Identify future postschool service needs using transition planning documents in conjunction with relevant agencies.

---

**TS:  Transition Specialists**
**8.  Professionalism and Ethical Practices**

*Knowledge:*

K1  Scope and role of a transition specialist.

K2  Scope and role of agency personnel related to transition-focused education and services.

*Skills:*

S1  Demonstrate positive regard for the capacity and operating constraints of community organizations involved in transition-focused education and services.

# CEC Knowledge and Skills for
# Beginning Special Education Paraeducators

## KNOWLEDGE AND SKILLS STATEMENTS

---

**PE:  Paraeducator Common Core**
**1.   Philosophical, Historical, and Legal Foundations of Special Education**

*Knowledge:*

K1  Purposes of programs for individuals with exceptionalities.

K2  Beliefs, traditions, and values across cultures and their effect on the relationships among children, families, and schooling.

K3  Rights and responsibilities of parents and children/youth as they relate to individual learning needs.

K4  The distinctions between roles and responsibilities of professionals, paraeducators, and support personnel.

*Skills:*

S1  Perform responsibilities under the supervision of a certified/licensed professional in a manner consistent with the requirements of law, rules and regulations, and local district policies and procedures.

---

**PE:  Paraeducator Common Core**
**2.   Characteristics of Learners**

*Knowledge:*

K1  Impact of differential characteristics of individuals with exceptionalities on the individual's life and family in the home, school, and community.

K2  Indicators of abuse and neglect that put students at risk.

*Skills:*

## PE: Paraeducator Common Core
## 3. Assessment, Diagnosis, and Evaluation

*Knowledge:*

K1 Rationale for assessment.

*Skills:*

S1 Demonstrate basic data collection techniques.

S2 With direction from a professional, make and document objective observations appropriate to the individual with exceptional learning needs.

## PE: Paraeducator Common Core
## 4. Instructional Content and Practice

*Knowledge:*

K1 Demands of various learning environments on individuals with exceptional learning needs.

K2 Basic instructional and remedial methods, techniques, and materials.

K3 Basic technologies appropriate to individuals with exceptional learning needs.

*Skills:*

S1 Establish and maintain rapport with learners.

S2 Use developmentally and age-appropriate strategies, equipment, materials, and technologies, as directed, to accomplish instructional objectives.

S3 Assist in adapting instructional strategies and materials according to the needs of the learner.

S4 Follow written plans, seeking clarification as needed.

## PE: Paraeducator Common Core
## 5. Supporting the Teaching and Learning Environment

*Knowledge:*

*Skills:*

S1 Assist in maintaining a safe, healthy learning environment that includes following prescribed policy and procedures.

S2 Use basic strategies and techniques for facilitating the integration of individuals with exceptional learning needs in various settings.

**Skills:**

S3   As directed by a certified/licensed professional, prepare and organize materials to support teaching and learning.

S4   Use strategies that promote the learner's independence.

---

## PE: Paraeducator Common Core
## 6. Managing Student Behavior and Social Interaction Skills

*Knowledge:*

K1   Rules and procedural safeguards regarding the management of behaviors of individuals with exceptional learning needs.

**Skills:**

S1   Demonstrate effective strategies for the management of behavior.

S2   Use appropriate strategies and techniques to increase the individual's self-esteem, self-awareness, self-control, self-reliance, and self-advocacy.

S3   Assist in modifying the learning environment to manage behavior.

S4   Collect and provide objective, accurate information to professionals, as appropriate.

S5   Use appropriate strategies and techniques in a variety of settings to assist in the development of social skills.

---

## PE: Paraeducator Common Core
## 7. Communication and Collaborative Partnerships

*Knowledge:*

K1   Characteristics of effective communication with children, youth, families, and school and community personnel.

K2   Common concerns of parents of individuals with exceptionalities.

**Skills:**

S1   Under the direction of a certified/licensed professional, use constructive strategies in working with individuals with exceptional learning needs, parents, and school and community personnel in various learning environments.

S2   Follow the instructions of the professional.

S3   Foster respectful and beneficial relationships between families and other school and community personnel.

S4   Participate as requested in conferences with families or primary caregivers as members of the educational team.

*Knowledge:*

K3 Roles of individuals with exceptionalities, parents, teachers, paraeducators, and other school and community personnel in planning an individualized program.

K4 Ethical practices for confidential communication about individuals with exceptionalities.

*Skills:*

S5 Use appropriate basic educational terminology regarding students, programs, roles, and instructional activities.

S6 Demonstrate sensitivity to diversity in cultural heritages, lifestyles, and value systems among children, youth, and families.

S7 Function in a manner that demonstrates the ability to use effective problem solving, engage in flexible thinking, employ appropriate conflict management techniques, and analyze one's own personal strengths and preferences.

---

# PE: Paraeducator Common Core
## 8. Professionalism and Ethical Practices

*Knowledge:*

K1 Personal cultural biases and differences that affect one's ability to work effectively with children, youth, families, and other team members.

K2 The paraeducator as a role model for individuals with exceptional learning needs.

*Skills:*

S1 Demonstrate commitment to assisting learners in achieving their highest potential.

S2 Function in a manner that demonstrates a positive regard for the distinctions among roles and responsibilities of paraeducators, professionals, and other support personnel.

S3 Function in a manner that demonstrates the ability to separate personal issues from one's responsibilities as a paraeducator.

S4 Demonstrate respect for the culture, religion, gender, and sexual orientation of individual students.

S5 Promote and maintain a high level of competence and integrity.

S6 Exercise objective and prudent judgment.

S7 Demonstrate proficiency in academic skills including oral and written communication.

S8 Engage in activities that promote paraeducators' knowledge and skill development.

S9 Engage in self-assessment activities.

S10 Accept and use constructive feedback.

S11 Practice within the context of the CEC Code of Ethics and other written standards and policies of the school or agency where they are employed.

# APPENDICES

# Appendix 1
## CEC Professional Standards
## Historic Events

| | |
|---|---|
| 1922 | The establishment of professional standards for the field of special education is declared as one of the fundamental aims of CEC. |
| 1962 | Professional Standards is the theme of the national convention. |
| 1963 | CEC purpose statement includes standards for professional personnel. |
| 1965 | CEC Conference on Professional Standards |
| 1966 | *Professional Standards for Personnel in the Education of Exceptional Children* is published. |
| 1976 | *Guidelines for Personnel in the Education of Exceptional Children* is published. CEC and the National Council for Teacher Accreditation (NCATE) form a partnership for approving training programs. |
| 1980 | CEC standards adopted by NCATE. |
| 1981 | CEC Delegate Assembly charges CEC to develop, promote, and implement preparation and certification standards, and a code of ethics. |
| 1982 | CEC called to establish and promote appropriate professional standards in the organization's mission statement. |
| 1983 | CEC adopts Code of Ethics, Standards for Professional Practice, Standards for the Preparation of Special Education Personnel, and Standards for Entry Into Professional Practice. The Professional Standard Committee is charged with their implementation. |
| 1984 | NCATE adopts CEC's revised standards. CATE adopts their "Redesign" where colleges and universities submit their folios to the respective professional organizations. |
| 1985 | NCATE adopts Guidelines for Program Approval of both basic and advanced special education preparation programs. |
| 1986 | CEC begins reviewing folios of programs seeking national accreditation. Guidelines for folio preparation adopted by CEC. |
| 1987 | *Standards and Guidelines for Curriculum Excellence in Personnel Preparation Programs in Special Education* is published |
| 1989 | CEC Delegate Assembly adopts policy framework for CEC Standards for Entry Into Professional Practice. |
| 1990 | NCATE adopts CEC's revised Guidelines for Program Approval of both basic and advanced special education preparation programs. |
| 1992 | CEC adopts the Common Core of Knowledge and Skills Essential for All Beginning Special Education Teachers.<br>CEC adopts non-NCATE Guidelines for Program Approval for IHEs including institutional, faculty, and program resources. |
| 1993 | CEC Standards for Entry Into Professional Practice are revised.<br>CEC revises non-NCATE Guidelines for Program Approval for IHEs including institutional, faculty, and program resources. |
| 1995 | CEC adopts initial areas of specialization knowledge and skill standards.<br>New standards published and submitted for NCATE adoption.<br>*What Every Special Educator Must Know: The International Standards for the Preparation and Certification of Special Education Teachers* is published. |
| 1996 | *What Every Special Educator Must Know: The International Standards for the Preparation and Certification of Special Education Teachers* (2nd edition) is published. |
| 1997 | CEC initiates the Professionally Recognized Special Educator, a national special education certification program with certificates for special education teachers, administrators, and diagnosticians. NCATE initiates the NCATE 2000 project to move to measuring performance in program accreditation. |
| 1998 | Knowledge and Skill Standards for Transition Specialists, Special Education Administrators, Education Diagnosticians, and Special Education Paraeducators are approved.<br>The Standards for Entry Into Professional Practice are revised. |

Guidelines for continuing education are approved.

Revisions to the Common Core of Knowledge and Skills Essential for All Beginning Special Education Teachers are approved.

The Curriculum Referenced Licensing and Program Accreditation Framework is approved.

*What Every Special Educator Must Know: The International Standards for the Preparation and Certification of Special Educators* (3rd edition) is published.

2001        CEC submits performance standards for NCATE approval.

# *Appendix 2*
## Development of and Procedures for Validating the Knowledge and Skills Standards

CEC carries out the development of professional standards through the Professional Standards and Practice Standing Committee (PSPSC) and its relevant subcommittees. One of the major responsibilities of the PSPSC has been the development, validation, and updating of the knowledge and skills bases in the various areas of special education.

### Development of the Standards
In 1989, the PSPSC established the first Knowledge and Skills Subcommittee (KSS), cochaired by Barbara Sirvis, of New York, and Bill Swan, of Georgia, and composed of CEC division representatives and past CEC Teachers of the Year. It set out to accomplish the following two major tasks:

- Identify a common core of knowledge and skills for all beginning special education teachers.
- Create specialty sets of knowledge and skills that are necessary to teach in a particular area of exceptionality or age group.

The KSS gathered materials from literature; state, provincial, and local governments; institutions of higher education; and elsewhere. The KSS then identified and organized thousands of competencies into major categories, culled them down to 195 statements, and determined the importance of each by surveying a 1,000-person sample of CEC's membership. Based on the response (54%), the KSS reduced the number of statements to 107.

CEC adopted these validated statements, which became The CEC Common Core of Knowledge and Skills Essential for All Beginning Special Education Teachers, published in the fall 1992 issue of *TEACHING Exceptional Children*.

Alan Koenig, of Texas, assumed the chairmanship of the KSS 1993 and began developing specialty sets of knowledge and skills to supplement the Common Core. The exceptionality and age-specific CEC divisions took the lead, developing sets of knowledge and skills necessary to teach in their areas of specialization. The KSS worked with the divisions to ensure that the specialty sets were formatted properly and that the statements supplemented the Common Core.

The KSS also developed a survey, which was sent to a random sample of the division's membership to validate the specialty sets. Each survey was sent to a sample of CEC members, half of whom were teachers and other direct service providers. Modifications were made in consultation with the division. Gener-

ally, there was a high level of concurrence with the work the division produced.

The Early Childhood Special Education specialization area knowledge and skills statements are taken from a concept paper, jointly approved by CEC's Division for Early Childhood (DEC), the National Association for the Education of Young Children (NAEYC), and the Association of Teacher Educators (ATE), Personnel Standards for Early Education and Early Intervention: Guidelines for Licensure in Early Childhood Special Education (DEC, NAEYC, & ATE, 1995). The content standards portion of the paper, however, has been reformatted to maintain consistency with CEC's eight categories of knowledge and skills statements for this publication. In its approved format, the concept paper included standards categories of (a) child development and learning, (b) curriculum development and implementation, (c) family and community relationships, (d) assessment and evaluation, (e) field experiences, and (f) professionalism. These six categories were selected to promote consistency with the NAEYC Guidelines for Preparation of Early Childhood Professionals (NAEYC, 1991) and to facilitate states' using the option to develop combined certifications. The concept paper in this latter format is disseminated by DEC, NAEYC, and ATE.

All of the performance standards, with the exception of the field experiences standards, were included and grouped under one of the eight CEC knowledge and skills category headings. The field experiences standards were incorporated into the CEC/NCATE Guidelines for CEC Program Approval of Undergraduate or Basic Programs. The reader should note that performance standards are based on the notion that the individual can demonstrate ability to perform in authentic situations. Although the emphasis is on performance, the implication is that individuals have the knowledge base to apply skills in specific situations. The performance standards, therefore, are grouped as skills. Because of this, knowledge statements are not included in the Early Childhood Special Education specialization section. It is important, however, to emphasize that the early childhood and early childhood special education knowledge bases support these skills statements.

In 1996, after initial publication of *What Every Special Educator Must Know*, comments were received from the field regarding the knowledge and skills statements. After review of all of the comments, CEC approved in the spring of 1996 a number of technical and clarifying changes. These were included in the second edition of this publication.

In 1998, the KSS, now chaired by Rachelle Bruno of Kentucky, began the process of developing the Curriculum Referenced Licensing and Program Accreditation Framework. This new framework was approved by the PSPSC in April 1998. The KSS also approved Knowledge and Skill sets for educational diagnosticians, special education administrators, and technology specialists.

The special education paraeducator knowledge and skills were approved in 1998 with the close collaboration of the National Resource Center for Paraeducators, the National Education Association, and the American Federation of Teachers.

### Procedures for the Validation of the Knowledge and Skills Standards

The following process is used for developing and validating knowledge and skills bases.

1. At least annually, the PSPSC determines which areas of knowledge and skills need to be developed, and sends these to the KSS.
2. In collaboration with relevant CEC divisions/units, the KSS gathers materials from literature; state, provincial, and local governments; institutions of higher education; and elsewhere.
3. The KSS then identifies and organizes the knowledge and skills statements into major categories.
4. The proposed knowledge and skills statements are included in a survey that is sent to a stratified random sample of the CEC membership with at least 50% of the sample being CEC members currently working in a position directly relevant to the knowledge and skills being validated.
5. Next, the KSS reviews the survey data, selects knowledge and skill statements validated by the survey, and submits their recommendations to the PSPSC.
6. The PSPSC reviews the recommendations from the KSS and makes a determination regarding the Knowledge and Skills.
7. The PSPSC communicates its decisions to the CEC Assistant Executive Director for Professional Standards and Practice and to the CEC Executive Board in an annual report.

The following validation process is used for amending the knowledge and skills bases.

1. Any member or recognized unit within CEC may recommend amendments to the knowledge and skills bases by submitting the request to the Assistant Executive Director for Professional Standards and Practice at CEC headquarters.
2. The PSPSC reviews the amendments and determines whether to consider them for validation or reject them.

3. If accepted, the proposed amendments are published in a CEC publication, and sent to the KSS for validation.
4. The KSS prepares a survey containing the proposed amendments and sends the survey to a stratified random sample of the CEC membership with at least 50% of the sample being CEC members currently working in a position directly relevant to the knowledge and skills.
5. The KSS reviews the survey data, selects the amended knowledge and skills statements validated by the survey, and submits these as recommendations to the PSPSC.
6. The PSPSC reviews the results of the process and makes a determination regarding the amendments.
7. The PSPSC communicates its decisions to the CEC Assistant Executive Director for Professional Standards and Practice and to the CEC Executive Board in an annual report.

Each process is overseen by the PSPSC. Originally, the areas of specialization were organized around categories of exceptionality, (e.g. learning disabilities, emotional and behavioral disorders). This does not indicate any CEC preference for categorical licensure or program accreditation. This was based on the leadership work of the categorical divisions within CEC. More recently, areas other than disability category have moved to the forefront, (e.g. technology, transition, diversity, administration, educational diagnostician, and special education paraeducators).

# Appendix 3

## Setting and Meeting Standards in Special Education*

*Frances P. Connor*

The founders of The Council for Exceptional Children (CEC) declared in 1922 that one of its primary purposes was to establish professional standards in the field of special education. This mission was a major step toward the development of special education into a profession.

What led to our founding? What teacher preparation programs were already in existence? What developments in supportive legislation, preservice education, and professional standards have occurred in our 75-year history? How has CEC contributed? This article briefly outlines some of the advances in the field and provides some perspective on the future.

### EDUCATIONAL OPPORTUNITIES FOR TEACHERS

Students of special education need no introduction to the early efforts of de L'Epee, Braille, Itard, Pereire, Seguin, Montessori, Bell, Gallaudet, and Howe and their influence on educational programs for exceptional children. In most instances, their followers—new teachers—learned their skills directly from their "masters." But other leaders initiated increasingly more formal instructions for teachers and potential teachers in the special classes and schools in which the children were taught.

In the late 19th century, educators and other professionals formed advocacy groups to improve the education and care of exceptional children. Some of these groups were the American Instructors of the Deaf (1849); the American Association of Instructors of the Blind (1871); the American Association on Mental Deficiency (1879); and the Alexander Graham Bell Association, devoted to oral education of deaf students (1890).

As special schools and classes expanded around the turn of the century, the need for teachers with specialized preparation grew. Those efforts were extended to school-based training programs, such as the "summer" session offerings at New Jersey's Vineland Training School, which included both preservice and inservice training of teachers of students with mental retardation. Penn State provided a summer session (1897) for teachers of "backward" children; the University of California (1918) initiated a program for the teachers of children who were blind; and a Department of Special Education was established at Miami University in Ohio (1919). Teachers College at Columbia University (1920), under Leta Hollingsworth, developed a program to prepare teach-

ers of gifted children. In 1917, the U.S. Office of Education (USOE) published data and lists of resources dealing with exceptional children. By 1929, USOE reported 43 training institutions offering special education courses.

In the spring 1925 issue of *The Crippled Child*, Michigan State Normal College advertised a 1-year course to prepare teachers of "crippled children," in an effort to counteract teacher shortages:

> The course is divided into periods of 12 weeks each, during which time a thorough acquaintance is made with their problems. . . . Four units of college credits will be covered each term, and the student . . . will be entitled to 1 year of college credit.

The program was weighted toward in-school experience.

In 1949, a national study of opportunities in institutions of higher education (IHEs) for special education teacher preparation (a cooperative effort of USOE and the National Society for Crippled Children and Adults, Inc.) set forth criteria for the preparation programs. The following were the three required program components:

- A study of the characteristics (physical, mental, and emotional) of the particular condition under consideration.
- A study of the teaching methods and curriculum adjustments needed.
- Observation and student teaching practice in the specialized area.

Mackie (1953-1958) identified 122 colleges or universities that in 1953-54 provided sequences of preparation in one or more areas of exceptionality. More colleges (115) offered programs for "speech correctionists" than for any of the other nine areas of specialization. There were more programs for preparing teachers of students with physical and mental disabilities than for teachers of students with emotional disturbance or gifted students. Colleges offered 68 program sequences for teachers of hard-of-hearing students and 22 for teachers of students who are deaf.

In all, the number of colleges and universities with a program sequence rose from 77 in 1949 to 122 in 1953-54—a minimum 58% increase (the former included summer offerings, the latter did not). The nation's total number of special education degrees granted in the participating colleges in 1953-1954 was 594, in areas other than speech.

The number of teacher preparation programs—and degrees granted—has exploded: In 1993-1994, about 900 colleges and universities offered degrees in special education, awarding 9,099 bachelor's degrees, 10,497 master's degrees, and 194 doctoral degrees. As the number of special educators grew in the 1960s, as well as the number and diversity of the college and university professional preparation programs, educators and policymakers paid increasing attention to the need for standards to guide the profession.

## SUPPORTIVE LEGISLATION

As publicly supported special education programs for exceptional students grew in number, and the types of students served diversified during the 1950s, schools demanded well-prepared special educators. Recognizing that the field first needed special education administrators, supervisors, and teacher educators, the U.S. Congress enacted Public Law 85-926 in 1958 to support fellowships in mental retardation that enabled special educators to return to school for advanced study. Public Law 87-276 was enacted in 1961 to support the preparation of teachers of students who were deaf, speech pathologists, and audiologists.

The last act President John F. Kennedy signed into law, before that fateful day in Dallas, was P.L. 88-164 (1963). One provision of this act consolidated and expanded federal preparation programs for special education professionals to include all areas of disabilities, as well as teachers and leadership professionals.

Through the 1960s and early 1970s, special education programs in schools and IHEs grew as qualified professionals were available or positions could be filled with unqualified personnel who were willing to become qualified by obtaining the necessary professional preparation. Because schools were not *required* to serve students with exceptionalities, and waiting lists for services were commonplace, services tended to become available when personnel could be employed.

This all changed in the latter half of the 1970s when Congress passed P.L. 94-142, the Education for All Handicapped Children Act of 1975. This act mandated that students with disabilities had a right to an education and appropriate special education and related services. Within a short time, demand for special educators outstripped the capability of the system to recruit, prepare, and retrain persons in careers in special education.

The mandates of P.L. 94-142 affected more than the demand for special educators. They also greatly affected what special educators had to know and be able to do. Students with "severe developmental disabilities," who had been considered by the educational system as "uneducable," were now to be educated. In a relatively short time, special education developed a body of knowledge on curriculums and methodologies for teaching such students, developed professional preparation programs, and prepared teachers and others for this new endeavor. Special educators had to know legal policies and procedures, how to work with other professionals, and how to work in more inclusive environments. Not only did the professional preparation programs have to retool to meet these new challenges, but *several hundred thousand* practicing special educators had to learn new knowledge and skills. Never had a field of education undergone such dramatic change in so short a time. Given that context, it is rather astounding at what was accomplished. Federal funds for personnel preparation, which continued to grow during this period, played a significant role by helping to support the development of curriculums for preparing special educators, the growth of professional preparation programs, and the costs incurred by people seeking degrees or certification in special education. If our field is to continue to grow and improve its practice, federal support for teacher and leadership professional preparation programs is essential.

## PROFESSIONAL STANDARDS

In 1965, CEC held a conference on professional standards at which participants drafted statements of standards. After revision, they were discussed in four regional conferences. Eventually, the Council's Delegate Assembly reviewed and approved the resulting standards. These early professional standards included directives to ensure a basic level of standards (mandates from the field) related to teachers' education programs, certification and accreditation, continuing education, special education doctoral programs, and ethics of behavior. In addition, specialists in each of the areas of exceptionality around which special education was organized had developed general guidelines for their specialists. Included were speech and hearing, deaf and hard of hearing, visually handicapped, the gifted, mentally retarded, behavioral disorders, physically handicapped, and administration and supervision. It was a noble beginning—our first statement of professional standards for the educator of exceptional children.

By 1972, however, only 6 years later, the field was changing rapidly and could not be bound by outdated guidelines. Changes in knowledge, philosophy, practice, and the problems presented by exceptional children being served in less restrictive settings were challenging. Thus, in revising the standards, CEC broadened its scope. A consultant to the process, Margaret Lindsay—a leader in teacher education and an active participant in the 1970 revision of the National Council for Accreditation of Teacher Education

(NCATE) standards—made it clear that we could not afford to be too constrictive or inflexible.

Concurrently, in September of 1970, the National Association of State Directors of Teacher Education and Certification became conscious of its limited consideration of exceptional children in their program-approval process. Because that organization was initiating a "Certification Reciprocity System" and needed to include special education, it was of increasing concern to CEC. Teacher mobility required certification across states, especially with a shortage of teachers in many regions of the United States.

The 1970s CEC Professional Standards and Guidelines Project, cochaired by Jean R. Hebler from the University of Maryland and Maynard Reynolds from the University of Minnesota, considered the needs of paraprofessionals and undergraduate and graduate-level preparation programs. Members discussed concepts, issues, and problems related to professional competencies and preparation programs. The resulting, broadly based standards encouraged focus on recruitment, selection, training and employment, program development, and evaluation. According to the report approved by the Delegate Assembly in 1975, CEC's local chapters reflected the sequence of socialization of personnel in the field—recruitment, selection of potential special educators, and retention of personnel. CEC also approved a continuing standards study.

In 1973, Maynard Reynolds conducted the Delphi Survey for the CEC Standards Committee to determine members' predictions and preferences related to recruitment, preparation, certification, and accreditation procedures. The approximately 1,150 responses showed considerable fervor over certification, calling especially for a reduction in the number of teaching certificates. They reflected a shift from *process* criteria to *performance* criteria; they supported strengthening the voluntary national and regional accreditation and focus on specific fields. The conclusions were discussed and debated during the continuing work on the CEC standards review. The work of the project was published in *Guidelines for Personnel in the Education of Exceptional Children* (CEC 1976).

In 1976, CEC became a member of NCATE. Oliver Hurley was appointed as CEC's representative, with Bill Carriker as an alternate. Hurley also was serving as chairman of CEC's Professional Standards Committee. Hurley expressed concern that CEC needed to further develop its guidelines because of growing pressure from NCATE. The following is an excerpt from his report to the CEC Board of Governors in January 1976:

> [There is] strong feeling to accredit by program (e.g., elementary education, art education, English education, special education, etc.) Or by

specialty areas within the programs. . . . This could result in some programs being accredited and others not being accredited within the same institution. This is a noteworthy trend. If realized, the *CEC Guidelines* will assume paramount importance for special education programs.

The CEC Professional Standards Committee then established a process to review and improve the guidelines and to involve CEC Divisions in the development of guidelines in specialty areas.

CEC activity during the late 1970s on professional standards reflects two major thrusts: first, the improvement of the guidelines; second, the strengthening and improvement of CEC's role in NCATE. These activities were primarily led by Bill Heller, who assumed the Chair of the Professional Standards Committee in 1979, and Bill Carriker, who was CEC's representative to NCATE. This process, which included significant collaboration efforts with the Teacher Education Division and the Higher Education Consortium for Special Education, led to the development of proposed CEC standards for NCATE adoption. These standards were approved by the CEC governance in 1980 and then by NCATE.

In 1981, the Virginia Federation of CEC proposed a resolution that was adopted by the CEC Delegate Assembly requiring CEC to develop, promote, and implement standards for preparing special educators, a code of ethics, standards of practice, and appropriate certification and licensure standards for the field.

After extensive member and CEC unit input, the CEC Delegate Assembly adopted a Code of Ethics and Standards for Professional Practice in 1983. During this same period, NCATE began to adopt what is commonly referred to as "redesign." Redesign not only changed the way the NCATE accreditation process works, but also significantly changed CEC's role. In this process, NCATE no longer reviews specific programs at an IHE, but rather focuses on the unit, that is, the *overall* operation of the school of education. NCATE then requires IHEs to submit their *specialty* programs to approved professional organizations, such as CEC. Thus, for special education, CEC is the recognized authority for standards. *These speciality reviews are paper (folio) reviews, and no site visit is conducted.*

In 1986, CEC began to review folios submitted from IHEs. The Professional Standards and Practices Standing Committee (PSPSC) soon realized that insufficient guidance was being provided to IHEs to know how to respond to a paper review. The committee developed more detailed guidelines, which NCATE adopted with an effective date of spring 1988.

In the late 1980s, CEC undertook the development of standards for the certification of entry-level special educators, to complete the mandate set by the CEC

Delegate Assembly in 1983. The CEC Professional Standards and Practice Standing Committee established a Certification Subcommittee under Bill Swan of the University of Georgia to develop the standards. Their first proposal, that entry into the profession based on a Master's degree in Special Education, was rejected by the Delegate Assembly. Based on the subcommittee's second recommendation, the Delegate Assembly adopted the following standard in 1989:

I. To be qualified to enter into practice as a special education teacher, an individual must possess no less than a bachelor's degree that encompasses the knowledge and skills consistent with the entry level into special education practice.

II. To be qualified to enter into practice as a special education teacher, an individual must possess the knowledge and skills set forth in the *CEC Common Core of Knowledge and Skills Essential for All Beginning Special Education Teachers.*

III. To be qualified to enter into practice as a special education teacher, an individual must possess the knowledge and skills set forth in at least one of the *CEC Specialized Knowledge and Skills Essential for Beginning Special Education Teachers.*

IV. Each new professional in special education should receive a minimum of a 1-year mentorship during the first year of his or her professional special education practice in a new role. The mentor should be an experienced professional in the same or a similar role, who can provide expertise and support on a continuing basis.

V. Approval of individuals for professional practice in the field of special education should be for a limited period of time with periodic renewal.

VI. Each professional in the field of educating individuals with exceptionalities (e.g., teachers, supervisors, administrators, college/university faculty) should participate in a minimum of 25 clock hours each year of planned, preapproved, organized, and recognized professional development activities related to his or her field of professional practice. Such activities may include a combination of professional development units, continuing education units, college/university course work, professional organization service (e.g., in CEC federations and chapters, divisions, subdivisions, and caucuses), professional workshops, special projects, or reading professional literature. Employing agencies should provide resources to enable each professional's continuing development.

Now CEC faced its biggest challenge: identifying the minimum knowledge and skills that entry level professionals require for practice in our field. The CEC Professional Standards and Practice Study Committee under the leadership of its chair Frances Connor, established a Knowledge and Skills Subcommittee composed of representatives from each of CEC's Divisions and winners of the CEC Teacher of the Year Award. Under the co-chairmanship of Barbara Sirvis and Bill Swan, the subcommittee set out to accomplish two major tasks:

- *Identify a common core of knowledge and skills for all beginning special education teachers.*
- *Create specialty sets of knowledge and skills that are necessary to teach in a particular area of exceptionality or age group.*

The subcommittee gathered materials from research literature; state, provincial, and local governments; IHEs; and elsewhere. The subcommittee then identified and organized thousands of competencies into major categories, culled them down to 195 statements, and determined the importance of each by surveying a 1,000-person sample of CEC's membership. Based on the response (54%), the subcommittee reduced the number of statements to 107.

CEC adopted these validated statements, which became *The CEC Common Core of Knowledge and Skills Essential for All Beginning Special Education Teachers,* published in the Fall 1992 issue of *TEACHING Exceptional Children.*

Alan Koenig, of Texas, assumed the chairmanship of the Subcommittee on Knowledge and Skills in 1993 and began developing specialty sets of knowledge and skills to supplement the Common Core. The exceptionality and age-specific CEC divisions took the lead, developing sets of knowledge and skills necessary to teach in their areas of specialization. The subcommittee worked with the divisions to ensure that the specialty sets were formatted properly and that the statements supplemented the Common Core.

The subcommittee also developed a survey, which was sent to a random sample of each division's membership. Each survey was composed of at least half teachers and other direct service providers. Modifications were made in consultation with the division. Generally, there was a high level of concurrence with the work the division produced.

CEC adopted specialization standards in 1995 and amended them in 1996. They were adopted by NCATE in 1996 and are now being used widely in the field. Work is now underway to develop knowledge- and skills-based standards for entry-level nonteaching special education professionals, such as administrators, technology specialists, educational diagnosticians, and career/transition specialists. The subcommittee is also developing standards for paraprofessionals.

CEC has now clearly established itself in the leadership role envisioned by its founders 75 years ago as the standard setter for the special education profession.

## Perspectives on the Road to Excellence

The story of special education has been one of social revolution. It reflects a powerful national move to include all children in an appropriate educational program. But the field continues to adjust and readjust its priorities, particularly its obligations to children and youth often excluded from education or diminished because of teacher attitudes or lack of competence.

Exceptional children have gained the right to an education. Its effectiveness depends on the knowledge, skill, and commitment of their teachers who, in turn, require teacher educators who are critical scholars with a broad understanding of and skill in the education of exceptional children, as well as in-depth command of a specialization. The curriculum for the preparation of special educators as reflected in CEC's *Standards for the Preparation and Certification of Teachers* is a clear indicator of the development of a profession. Basic to the standards for entry into the field is the *Code of Ethics,* originally adopted by the Council's Delegate Assembly in 1983. Adopted also were the standards of professional practice, specifying areas of responsibility and professional behavior to ensure quality education for all people with exceptionalities. These areas of commitment are as follows:

- Instructional responsibilities.
- Management of behavior.
- Support procedures.
- Parental relationships.
- Professional employment.
- Professionals in relation to other professionals.

The CEC standards are designed for entry level into the profession. We now need to put them into the context of a total program for the preparation and practice of the profession at all levels including career teachers, experienced senior teachers who also requires renewal prior to assuming the highly responsible role of mentoring, and college personnel responsible for building competence in working interns. The apparent isolation or autonomy of college instructors or professors urgently needs revision. Their entry into the profession and experience in teaching exceptional children may be decades removed from their present responsibilities in IHE classrooms or in supervision of the practice of prospective or novice teachers. Who will certify them? Who will supervise them?

As the field emerges more fully as a profession, its teachers must be broadly educated in the arts and sciences, preferably prior to entering professional preparation. With the changing child populations, they require a strong knowledge and practicum base across the specializations. But a cross-categorical preparation for a "special educator" or for the general classroom teacher to instruct any and all highly exceptional children seems doomed to instructional mediocrity. Do not parents of children with unique problems merit teachers with deep understanding and specialized information based on academic research and clinical studies of practice? Is it not possible to have teams of special education teachers with in-depth knowledge of various specializations work together to provide the content, technical competence, and demonstration of instructional modifications to permit the child to reach his or her potential? Why should we be satisfied when students meet only minimum requirements for graduation (or "completion") and have access only to sheltered or minimum-wage jobs?

We have made outstanding progress in including all children. But accumulation of college credits, student theses/dissertations, and a record of practicum classroom teaching do not a competent teacher educator make.

Becoming a profession is not enough. The standards development must continue, and teacher education institutions must change. Each exceptional child and each teacher is entitled to an education for excellence.

*Frances P. Connor* (CEC New Jersey Federation), Retired Professor and Chair Department of Special Education, Columbia University, New York, New York. She served as Chair of CEC's Professional Standards and Practice Study Committee.

### Resources

For further discussion on the development of a profession and on teacher education, see the following publications.

The Council for Exceptional Children. (1966). *Professional standards for personnel in the education of exceptional children.* Reston, VA: Author. (ERIC Document Reproduction Service No. ED 017 085)

The Council for Exceptional Children. (1976). *Guidelines for personnel in the education of exceptional children.* Reston, VA: Author. (ERIC Document Reproduction Service No. ED 121 018)

The Council for Exceptional Children. (1983). *Standards for the preparation of special education personnel.* Reston, VA: Author.

The Council for Exceptional Children. (1995, 1996). *What every special educator must know: The international standards for the preparation and certification of special education teachers.* Reston, VA: Author.

Cremin, L. A. (1970-1988). *American education* (3 vols, covering the years 1607 to 1980). New York: Harper & Row.

Fearn, K. M. (1987). *Report on the status of certification of special educators in the United States and territories.* Reston, VA: CEC.

Guskey, T. R., & Huberman, M. (Eds.). (1995). *Professional development in education: New paradigms and practices.* New York: Teachers College Press, Teachers College, Columbia University.

The Holmes Group. (1986). *Tomorrow's teachers: A report of the Holmes Group.* East Lansing, MI: Author. (Available through the Holmes Group Inc., 501 Erikson Hall, East Lansing, MI 48824-1034.)

Jordan, J. (Ed.). (1977). *Exceptional child education at the bicentennial: A parade of progress.* Reston, VA: CEC. (ERIC Document Reproduction Service No. ED 172 500)

*Journal of the Teacher Education Division of the Council for Exceptional Children.* (1995, Summer). (Issue on doctoral and post-doctoral preparation.)

Mackie, R. (1953-1958). *Professional preparation of teachers of exceptional children* (13 reports from the study Qualifications and Preparation of Teachers of Exceptional Children). Washington, DC: U.S. Office of Education.

Reforming teacher education: A symposium on the Holmes Group Report. (1987, Spring). *Teachers College Record, 88*(3).

Rosenberg, M. S., & Rock, E. E. (1994). Alternate certification in special education: Efficacy of a field-based teacher preparation program. *Journal of the Teacher Education Division of the Council for Exceptional Children, 17*(3), 141-153.

Schofer, R. C., & McGough, R. L. (1977). *Manpower planning for special education: Planning model and alternatives.* Columbia: University of Missouri-Columbia. (ERIC Document Reproduction Service No. ED 228 805)

Southern Regional Educational Board. (1950s-1960s). [Reports on reciprocal certification of teachers and the improvement of teacher education]. Atlanta, GA: Author.

Weintraub, F. J., Abeson, A., Ballard, J., & LaVor, M. L. (1977). *Public policy and the education of exceptional children.* Reston, VA: CEC. [ERIC Document Reproduction Service No. ED 116 403]

*Adapted from Connor, F. P. (1997). Setting and Meeting Standards in Special Education. *TEACHING Exceptional Children, 29*(5), 27-33.

# *Appendix 4*
## Self-Evaluation for Students Preparing to Become Special Education Teachers

Appendix 4 is a self-evaluation instrument designed to be used by students of special education to evaluate their progress in learning the knowledge and skills they will need upon graduation from the preparation program. Students can use it in a variety of ways. Students can check off each knowledge and skill competency as they are acquired; they can also include the course number, as well as the specific activity that they completed.

Several colleges and universities have used a similar instrument for their students to self-evaluate their mastery of the CC standards periodically throughout their preparation program, including during their first year of teaching. This has some nice data for the preparation program that can be used to improve the program.

The only matrix included in this Appendix in the CEC Common Core, only because page limitations have prevented us from including Area of Specialization matrices. Similar matrices for each Area of Specialization could easily be prepared using the same format.

| Guidelines | Cite the course number and/or course lecture or activity in which each standard was mastered. |
|---|---|
| **CC:** **Common Core** **1.** **Philosophical, Historical, and Legal Foundations of Special Education** | |
| *Knowledge:* | |
| K1 Models, theories, and philosophies that provide the basis for special education practice. | |
| K2 Variations in beliefs, traditions, and values across cultures within society and the effect of the relationship among child, family, and schooling. | |
| K3 Issues in definition and identification procedures for individuals with exceptional learning needs including individuals from culturally and/or linguistically diverse backgrounds. | |
| K4 Issues, assurances and due process rights related to assessment, eligibility, and placement within a continuum of services. | |
| K5 Rights and responsibilities of parents, students, teachers and other professionals, and schools as they relate to individual learning needs. | |
| *Skills:* | |
| S1 Articulate personal philosophy of special education including its relationship to/with regular education. | |
| S2 Conduct instructional and other professional activities consistent with the requirements of law, rules and regulations, and local district policies and procedures. | |
| **CC:** **Common Core** **2.** **Characteristics of Learners** | |
| *Knowledge:* | |
| K1 Similarities and differences among the cognitive, physical, cultural, social, and emotional needs of individuals with and without exceptional learning needs. | |

| | Guidelines | Cite the course number and/or course lecture or activity in which each standard was mastered. |
|---|---|---|
| K2 | Differential characteristics of individuals with exceptionalities, including levels of severity and multiple exceptionalities. | |
| K3 | Characteristics of normal, delayed, and disordered communication patterns of individuals with exceptional learning needs. | |
| K4 | Effects an exceptional condition(s) may have on an individual's life. | |
| K5 | Characteristics and effects of the cultural and environmental milieu of the child and the family including cultural and linguistic diversity, socioeconomic level, abuse/neglect, and substance abuse. | |
| K6 | Effects of various medications on the educational, cognitive, physical, social, and emotional behavior of individuals with exceptionalities. | |
| K7 | Educational implications of characteristics of various exceptionalities. | |
| *Skills:* | | |
| S1 | Access information on various cognitive, communication, physical, cultural, social, and emotional conditions of individuals with exceptional learning needs. | |
| CC: 3. | **Common Core** **Assessment, Diagnosis, and Evaluation** | |
| *Knowledge:* | | |
| K1 | Basic terminology used in assessment. | |
| K2 | Ethical concerns related to assessment. | |
| K3 | Legal provisions, regulations, and guidelines regarding assessment of individuals. | |
| K4 | Typical procedures used for screening, prereferral, referral, and classification. | |

| | Guidelines | Cite the course number and/or course lecture or activity in which each standard was mastered. |
|---|---|---|
| K5 | Appropriate application and interpretation of scores, including grade score versus standard score, percentile ranks, age/grade equivalents, and stanines. | |
| K6 | Appropriate use and limitations of each type of assessment instrument. | |
| K7 | Incorporation of strategies that consider the influence of diversity on assessment, eligibility, programming, and placement of individuals with exceptional learning needs. | |
| K8 | The relationship between assessment and placement decisions. | |
| K9 | Methods for monitoring progress of individuals with exceptional learning needs. | |
| Skills: | | |
| S1 | Collaborate with families and other professionals involved in the assessment of individuals with exceptional learning needs. | |
| S2 | Create and maintain records. | |
| S3 | Gather background information regarding academic, medical, and family history. | |
| S4 | Use various types of assessment procedures appropriately. | |
| S5 | Interpret information from formal and informal assessment instruments and procedures. | |
| S6 | Report assessment results to individuals with exceptional learning needs, parents, administrators, and other professionals using appropriate communication skills. | |
| S7 | Use performance data and information from teachers, other professionals, individuals with exceptionalities, and parents to make or suggest appropriate modification in learning environments. | |

| | Guidelines | Cite the course number and/or course lecture or activity in which each standard was mastered. |
|---|---|---|
| S8 | Develop individualized assessment strategies for instruction. | |
| S9 | Use assessment information in making instructional decisions and planning individual programs that result in appropriate placement and intervention for all individuals with exceptional learning needs, including those from culturally and/or linguistically diverse backgrounds. | |
| S10 | Evaluate the results of instruction. | |
| S11 | Evaluate supports needed for integration into various program placements. | |
| CC: 4. | **Common Core** **Instructional Content and Practice** | |
| *Knowledge:* | | |
| K1 | Differing learning styles of individuals with exceptional learning needs and how to adapt teaching to these styles. | |
| K2 | Demands of various learning environments such as individualized instruction in general education classes. | |
| K3 | Curricula for the development of motor, cognitive, academic, social, language, affective, career, and functional life skills for individuals with exceptional learning needs. | |
| K4 | Instructional and remedial methods, techniques, and curriculum materials. | |
| K5 | Techniques for modifying instructional methods and materials. | |
| K6 | Life skills instruction relevant to independent, community, and personal living and employment. | |

| | Guidelines | Cite the course number and/or course lecture or activity in which each standard was mastered. |
|---|---|---|
| K7 | Cultural perspectives influencing the relationship among families, schools, and communities as related to effective instruction for individuals with exceptional learning needs. | |
| K8 | Impact of learners' attitudes, interests, values and academic and social abilities on intervention, instructional planning and career development. | |
| **Skills:** | | |
| S1 | Interpret and use assessment data for instruction. | |
| S2 | Develop and/or select instructional content, materials, resources, and strategies that respond to cultural, linguistic, and gender differences. | |
| S3 | Develop comprehensive, longitudinal individualized programs. | |
| S4 | Choose and use appropriate technologies to accomplish instructional objectives and to integrate them appropriately into the instructional process. | |
| S5 | Prepare appropriate lesson plans. | |
| S6 | Involve the individual and family in setting instructional goals and charting progress. | |
| S7 | Use task analysis. | |
| S8 | Select, adapt, and use instructional strategies and materials according to characteristics of the learner. | |
| S9 | Sequence, implement, and evaluate individual learning objectives. | |
| S10 | Integrate affective, social, and career/vocational skills with academic curricula. | |
| S11 | Use strategies for facilitating maintenance and generalization of skills across learning environments. | |

| | Guidelines | Cite the course number and/or course lecture or activity in which each standard was mastered. |
|---|---|---|
| S12 | Use instructional time properly. | |
| S13 | Teach individuals with exceptional learning needs to use thinking, problem-solving, and other cognitive strategies to meet their individual needs. | |
| S14 | Choose and implement instructional techniques and strategies that promote successful transitions for individuals with exceptional learning needs. | |
| S15 | Establish and maintain rapport with learners. | |
| S16 | Use verbal and nonverbal communication techniques. | |
| S17 | Conduct self-evaluation of instruction. | |
| S18 | Make immediate responsive adjustments to instructional strategies based on continual observations. | |
| **CC: 5.** | **Common Core Planning and Managing the Teaching and Learning Environment** | |
| *Knowledge:* | | |
| K1 | Basic classroom management theories, methods, and techniques for individuals with exceptional learning needs. | |
| K2 | Research-based best practices for effective management of teaching and learning. | |
| K3 | Ways in which technology can assist with planning and managing the teaching and learning environment. | |
| *Skills:* | | |
| S1 | Create a safe, positive, and supportive learning environment in which diversities are valued. | |
| S2 | Use strategies and techniques for facilitating the functional integration of individuals with exceptional learning needs in various settings. | |

| | Guidelines | *Cite the course number and/or course lecture or activity in which each standard was mastered.* |
|---|---|---|
| S3 | Prepare and organize materials to implement daily lesson plans. | |
| S4 | Incorporate evaluation, planning, and management procedures that match learner needs with the instructional environment. | |
| S5 | Design a learning environment that encourages active participation by learners in a variety of individual and group learning activities. | |
| S6 | Design, structure, and manage daily routines, effectively including transition time, for students, other staff, and the instructional setting. | |
| S7 | Direct the activities of a classroom volunteer or peer tutor. | |
| S8 | Direct, observe, evaluate, and provide feedback to paraeducator. | |
| S9 | Create an environment that encourages self-advocacy and increased independence. | |
| S10 | Maintain a safe environment where universal precautions are practiced. | |
| **CC:** **6.** | **Common Core** **Managing Student Behavior and Social Interaction Skills** | |
| *Knowledge:* | | |
| K1 | Applicable laws, rules and regulations, and procedural safeguards regarding the planning and implementation of management of behaviors of individuals with exceptional learning needs. | |
| K2 | Ethical considerations inherent in behavior management. | |
| K3 | Teacher attitudes and behaviors that positively or negatively influence behavior of individuals with exceptional learning needs. | |

| | Guidelines | Cite the course number and/or course lecture or activity in which each standard was mastered. |
|---|---|---|
| K4 | Social skills needed for educational and functional living and working environments and effective instruction in the development of social skills. | |
| K5 | Strategies for crisis prevention/intervention. | |
| K6 | Strategies for preparing individuals to live harmoniously and productively in a multiclass, multiethnic, multicultural, and multinational world. | |
| **Skills:** | | |
| S1 | Demonstrate a variety of effective behavior management techniques appropriate to the needs of individuals with exceptional learning needs. | |
| S2 | Implement the least intensive intervention consistent with the needs of the individuals with exceptionalities. | |
| S3 | Modify the learning environment (schedule and physical arrangement) to manage inappropriate behaviors. | |
| S4 | Identify realistic expectations for personal and social behavior in various settings. | |
| S5 | Integrate social skills into the curriculum. | |
| S6 | Use effective teaching procedures in social skills instruction. | |
| S7 | Demonstrate procedures to increase the individual's self-awareness, self-management, self-control, self-reliance, and self-esteem. | |
| S8 | Prepare individuals with exceptional learning needs to exhibit self-enhancing behavior in response to societal attitudes and actions. | |
| **CC: 7.** | **Common Core Communication and Collaborative Partnerships** | |
| **Knowledge:** | | |

| | Guidelines | *Cite the course number and/or course lecture or activity in which each standard was mastered.* |
|---|---|---|
| K1 | Factors that promote effective communication and collaboration with individuals, parents, and school and community personnel in a culturally responsive program. | |
| K2 | Typical concerns of parents of individuals with exceptional learning needs and appropriate strategies to help parents deal with these concerns. | |
| K3 | Development of individual student programs working in collaboration with team members. | |
| K4 | Roles of individuals with exceptionalities, parents, teachers, and other school and community personnel in planning an individualized program. | |
| K5 | Ethical practices for confidential communication to others about individuals with exceptional learning needs. | |
| K6 | Roles and responsibilities of the pareducator related to instruction, intervention and direct services. | |
| K7 | Family systems and the role of families in supporting child development and educational progress. | |
| *Skills:* | | |
| S1 | Use collaborative strategies in working with individuals with exceptional learning needs, parents, and school and community personnel in various learning environments. | |
| S2 | Communicate and consult with individuals, parents, teachers, and other school and community personnel. | |
| S3 | Foster respectful and beneficial relationships between families and professionals. | |

| | Guidelines | *Cite the course number and/or course lecture or activity in which each standard was mastered.* |
|---|---|---|
| S4 | Encourage and assist individuals with exceptional learning needs and their families to become active participants in the educational team. | |
| S5 | Plan and conduct collaborative conferences with individuals with exceptional learning needs and families or primary caregivers. | |
| S6 | Collaborate with regular classroom teachers and other school and community personnel in integrating individuals with exceptional learning needs into various learning environments. | |
| S7 | Communicate with regular teachers, administrators, and other school personnel about characteristics and needs of individuals with specific exceptional learning needs. | |
| **CC: 8.** | **Common Core Professionalism and Ethical Practices** | |
| *Knowledge:* | | |
| K1 | Personal cultural biases and differences that affect one's teaching. | |
| K2 | Importance of the teacher serving as a model for individuals with exceptional learning needs. | |
| *Skills:* | | |
| S1 | Demonstrate commitment to developing the highest educational and quality-of-life potential of individuals with exceptional learning needs. | |
| S2 | Demonstrate positive regard for the culture, religion, gender, and sexual orientation of individual students. | |
| S3 | Promote and maintain a high level of competence and integrity in the practice of the profession. | |

| | Guidelines | Cite the course number and/or course lecture or activity in which each standard was mastered. |
|---|---|---|
| S4 | Exercise objective professional judgment in the practice of the profession. | |
| S5 | Demonstrate proficiency in oral and written communication. | |
| S6 | Engage in professional activities that may benefit individuals with exceptional learning needs, their families, and/or colleagues. | |
| S7 | Comply with local, state, provincial, and federal monitoring and evaluation requirements. | |
| S8 | Use copyrighted educational materials in an ethical manner. | |
| S9 | Practice within the CEC Code of Ethics and other standards and policies of the profession. | |

| Guidelines | Cite the course number and/or course lecture or activity in which each standard was mastered. |
|---|---|
| **GC:**    **Individualized General Curriculum Referenced Standards** | |
| **GC:**    **General Curriculum** <br> **1.**    **Foundations** | |
| *Knowledge:* | |
| K1    Current educational terminology and definitions of individuals with disabilities* including the identification criteria and labeling controversies, using professionally accepted classification systems, and current incidence and prevalence figures. | |
| K2    Evolution and major perspectives from medicine, psychology, behavior, and education on the definitions and etiologies of individuals with disabilities*. | |
| K3    Differing perceptions of deviance, including those from mental health, religion, legal-corrections, education, and social welfare. | |
| K4    The historical foundations, philosophies, theories and classic studies including the major contributors, and major legislation that undergird the growth and improvement of knowledge and practice in the field of special education. | |
| K5    The legal system to assist individuals with disabilities*. | |
| K6    Continuum of placement and services, including alternative programs available for individuals with disabilities*. | |
| K7    Laws, regulations, and policies related to the provision of specialized health care in the educational setting. | |
| *Skills:* | |
| S1    Articulate the pros and cons of current issues and trends in the education of individuals with disabilities*. | |
| S2    Articulate the factors that influence the overrepresentation of culturally/linguistically diverse students in programs for individuals with disabilities*. | |
| S3    Delineate the principles of normalization versus the educational concept of "least restrictive environment" in designing educational programs for individuals with disabilities*. | |

| Guidelines | Cite the course number and/or course lecture or activity in which each standard was mastered. |
|---|---|
| **GC: General Curriculum**<br>**2. Characteristics of Learners** | |
| *Knowledge:* | |
| K1 | Physical development, physical disabilities, and health impairments as they relate to the development and behavior of individuals with disabilities*. | |
| K2 | Effects of dysfunctional behavior on learning, and the differences between behavioral and emotional disorders and other disabling conditions. | |
| K3 | Various etiologies and medical aspects of conditions affecting individuals with disabilities*. | |
| K4 | Psychological and social-emotional characteristics of individuals with disabilities*. | |
| K5 | Common etiologies and the impact of sensory disabilities on learning and experience. | |
| *Skills:* | |
| S1 | Describe and define general developmental, academic, social, career, and functional characteristics of individuals with disabilities* as they relate to levels of support needed. | |
| **GC: General Curriculum**<br>**3. Assessment, Diagnosis, & Evaluation** | |
| *Knowledge:* | |
| K1 | Specialized terminology used in the assessment of individuals with disabilities*. | |
| K2 | Legal provisions, regulations, and guidelines regarding unbiased assessment and use of psychometric instruments and instructional assessment measures with individuals with disabilities*. | |
| K3 | Specialized policies regarding screening, referral, and placement procedures for individuals with disabilities*. | |
| *Skills:* | |
| S1 | Implement procedures for assessing and reporting both appropriate and problematic social behaviors of individuals with disabilities*. | |
| S2 | Use exceptionality-specific assessment instruments with individuals with disabilities*. | |
| S3 | Adapt and modify ecological inventories, | |

| Guidelines | Cite the course number and/or course lecture or activity in which each standard was mastered. |
|---|---|
| portfolio assessments, functional assessments, and future-based assessments to accommodate the unique abilities and needs of individuals with disabilities*. | |
| S4  Develop and use a technology plan based on assistive technology assessment. | |
| S5  Assess reliable method(s) of response of individuals who lack typical communication and performance abilities. | |
| **GC:  General Curriculum** **4.  Instructional Content & Practice** | |
| *Knowledge:* | |
| K1  Sources of specialized materials for individuals with disabilities*. | |
| K2  Impact of listening skills on the development of critical thinking, reading comprehension, and oral and written language. | |
| K3  Impact of language development on the academic and social skills of individuals with disabilities*. | |
| K4  Impact of disabilities on auditory skills. | |
| K5  Relationship between disabilities and reading instruction. | |
| K6  Impact of social skills on the lives of individuals with disabilities*. | |
| K7  Varied test-taking strategies. | |
| K8  Alternatives for teaching skills and strategies to individuals with learning disabilities who differ in degree and kind of disability. | |
| K9  Approaches to create positive learning environments for individuals with disabilities*. | |
| *Skills:* | |
| S1  Use effective, research-based instructional strategies and practices to meet the needs of individuals with disabilities*. | |
| S2  acilitate use of prevention and intervention strategies in educational settings. | |
| S3  Delineate and apply the goals, intervention strategies, and procedures related to psychodynamic, behavioral, biophysical, and ecological approaches to individuals with disabilities*. | |

| | Guidelines | Cite the course number and/or course lecture or activity in which each standard was mastered. |
|---|---|---|
| S4 | Plan, organize, and implement educational programs appropriate to the cognitive and affective needs of individuals with disabilities*. | |
| S5 | Evaluate, select, develop, and adopt curriculum materials and technology appropriate for individuals with disabilities*. | |
| S6 | Integrate academic instruction, affective education, and behavior management for individual learners and groups of learners. | |
| S7 | Evaluate strengths and limitations of alternative instructional strategies for individuals with disabilities*. | |
| S8 | Integrate student-initiated learning experiences into ongoing instruction. | |
| S9 | Use skills to enhance thinking processes. | |
| S10 | Use effective instructional strategies to assist individuals with disabilities* to detect and correct errors in oral and written language. | |
| S11 | Use appropriate instructional strategies to teach math skills and concepts according to the characteristics of the learner and patterns of error. | |
| S12 | Modify pace of instruction and use organization cues. | |
| S13 | Integrate appropriate teaching strategies and instructional approaches to provide effective instruction in academic and nonacademic areas for individuals with disabilities*. | |
| S14 | Utilize research-supported instructional strategies and practices, including the functional embedded skills approach, community-based instruction, task analysis, multisensory, and concrete/manipulative techniques. | |
| S15 | Design age-appropriate instruction based on the adaptive skills of learners. | |
| S16 | Integrate related services into the instructional settings of learners. | |
| S17 | Provide community referenced instruction. | |
| S18 | Assist students in the use of alternative and augmentative communication systems. | |
| S19 | Support the use of media, materials, alternative communication styles and resources required for learners whose disabilities interfere with | |

| Guidelines | Cite the course number and/or course lecture or activity in which each standard was mastered. |
|---|---|
| communications. | |
| S20 Interpret sensory, mobility, reflex, and perceptual information to create appropriate learning plans. | |
| S21 Use appropriate adaptations and technology for all individuals with disabilities*. | |
| S22 Adapt lessons that minimize the physical exertion of individuals with specialized health care needs. | |
| S23 Design and implement an instructional program that addresses instruction in independent living skills, vocational skills, and career education for students with physical and health disabilities emphasizing positive self-concepts and realistic goals. | |
| S24 Design and implement curriculum and instructional strategies for medical self-management procedures for students with specialized health care needs. | |
| S25 Participate in the selection and implementation of augmentative or alternative communication devices and systems for use with students with physical and health disabilities. | |
| S26 Use strategies for facilitating the maintenance and generalization of skills across learning environments. | |
| **GC: General Curriculum**<br>**5. Planning and Managing the Teaching and Learning Environment** | |
| *Knowledge:* | |
| K1 Model career, vocational, and transition programs for individuals with disabilities*. | |
| K2 Issues, resources, and techniques used to integrate students with disabilities into and out of special centers, psychiatric hospitals, and residential treatment centers. | |
| K3 Appropriate use of assistive devices to meet the needs of individuals with disabilities*. | |
| K4 Common environmental and personal barriers that hinder accessibility and acceptance of individuals with disabilities*. | |
| *Skills:* | |
| S1 Monitor intragroup behavior changes across | |

| | Guidelines | *Cite the course number and/or course lecture or activity in which each standard was mastered.* |
|---|---|---|
| | subjects and activities. | |
| S2 | Structure the educational environment to provide optimal learning opportunities for individuals with disabilities*. | |
| S3 | Teach individuals with disabilities* in a variety of educational settings. | |
| S4 | Design learning environments for individuals with disabilities* that provide feedback from peers and adults. | |
| S5 | Design learning environments that are multisensory and that facilitate active participation, self-advocacy, and independence of individuals with disabilities* in a variety of group and individual learning activities. | |
| S6 | Use local, community, state, and provincial resources to assist in programming with individuals who are likely to make progress in the general curriculum. | |
| S7 | Coordinate activities of related services personnel to maximize direct instruction time for individuals with disabilities*. | |
| **GC: 6.** | **General Curriculum Managing Student Behavior and Social Interaction Skills** | |
| *Knowledge:* | | |
| K1 | Rationale for selecting specific management techniques for individuals with disabilities*. | |
| K2 | Theories behind reinforcement techniques and their application to teaching individuals with disabilities*. | |
| K3 | Theories of behavior problems in individuals with disabilities*, including self-stimulation and self-abuse. | |
| K4 | Communication and social interaction alternatives for individuals who are nonspeaking. | |
| *Skills:* | | |
| S1 | Use a variety of nonaversive techniques for the purpose of controlling targeted behavior and maintaining attention of individuals with disabilities*. | |
| S2 | Develop and implement a systematic behavior management plan using observation, recording, | |

| | Guidelines | *Cite the course number and/or course lecture or activity in which each standard was mastered.* |
|---|---|---|
| | charting, establishment of timelines, hierarchies of interventions, and schedules of reinforcement. | |
| S3 | Select target behaviors to be changed and identify the critical variables affecting the target behavior. | |
| S4 | Define and use skills in problem-solving and conflict resolution. | |
| S5 | Design, implement, and evaluate instructional programs that enhance an individual's social participation in family, school, and community activities. | |
| S6 | Establish a consistent classroom routine for individuals with disabilities*. | |
| S7 | Delineate and apply appropriate management procedures when presented with spontaneous management problems. | |
| S8 | Facilitate development and implementation of rules and appropriate consequences in the educational environment. | |
| GC: 7. | **General Curriculum Communication and Collaborative Partnerships** | |
| *Knowledge:* | | |
| K1 | Sources of unique services, networks, and organizations for individuals with disabilities*, including career, vocational, and transition support. | |
| K2 | Parent education programs and behavior management guides, including those commercially available, that address the management of severe behavioral problems and facilitate communication links applicable to individuals with disabilities*. | |
| K3 | Collaborative and consultative roles of special education teachers in the integration of individuals with disabilities* into the general curriculum and classroom. | |
| K4 | Types and importance of information generally available from family, school officials, legal system, community service agencies. | |
| K5 | Roles and responsibilities of school-based medical and related services personnel, professional groups, and community organizations in identifying, assessing, and | |

| Guidelines | Cite the course number and/or course lecture or activity in which each standard was mastered. |
|---|---|
| providing services to individuals with disabilities*. | |
| *Skills:* | |
| S1 Use specific behavioral management and counseling techniques in managing students and providing training for their parents. | |
| S2 Assist students, in collaboration with parents and other professionals, in planning for transition to post-school settings with maximum opportunities for decision making and full participation in the community. | |
| GC: **General Curriculum**<br>8. **Professionalism and Ethical Practices** | |
| *Knowledge:* | |
| K1 Consumer and professional organizations, publications, and journals relevant to individuals with disabilities*. | |
| K2 Rights to privacy, confidentiality, and respect for differences among all persons interacting with individuals with disabilities*. | |
| K3 Types and transmission routes of infectious disease. | |
| K4 Maintain confidentiality of medical and academic records and respect for privacy of individuals with disabilities*. | |
| *Skills:* | |
| S1 Participate in the activities of professional organizations relevant to individuals with disabilities*. | |
| S2 Articulate the teacher's ethical responsibility to nonidentified individuals who function similarly to individuals with disabilities*. | |

*Implicit to all of the knowledge and skills standards in this section is the focus on individuals with disabilities whose education focuses on an individualized general curriculum.

| | Guidelines | Cite the course number and/or course lecture or activity in which each standard was mastered. |
|---|---|---|
| **IC:** | **Individualized Independence Curriculum Referenced Standards** | |
| **IC: 1.** | **Independence Curriculum Foundations** | |
| *Knowledge:* | | |
| K1 | Current educational terminology and definitions of individuals who would benefit most from an independence curriculum, including the identification criteria and labeling controversies, utilizing professional accepted classification systems and current incidence and prevalence figures. | |
| K2 | Evolution and major perspectives from medicine, psychology, behavior, and education on the definitions and etiologies of individuals with disabilities*. | |
| K3 | The historic foundations, classic studies including the major contributors, and major legislation that grounds the growth and improvement of knowledge and practice in the field of education of individuals with disabilities*. | |
| K4 | Continuum of placement and services available for individuals with disabilities*. | |
| K5 | Laws, regulations, and policies related to the provision of specialized health care in the educational setting. | |
| *Skills:* | | |
| S1 | Articulate the pros and cons of current issues and trends in the education of individuals with disabilities*. | |
| S2 | Delineate the principles of normalization versus the educational concept of "least restrictive environment" in designing educational programs for individuals with disabilities*. | |
| **IC: 2.** | **Independence Curriculum Characteristics of Learners** | |
| *Knowledge:* | | |
| K1 | Physical development, physical disabilities, sensory disabilities, and health impairments as they relate to the development and behavior of individuals who would benefit most from a functional independence curriculum. | |
| K2 | The various etiologies and medical aspects of | |

| | Guidelines | Cite the course number and/or course lecture or activity in which each standard was mastered. |
|---|---|---|
| | conditions affecting individuals with disabilities*. | |
| K3 | Psychological and social-emotional characteristics of individuals with disabilities*. | |
| K4 | Medical complications and implications for student support needs, including seizure management, tube feeding, catheterization, and cardiopulmonary resuscitation (CPR). | |
| **Skills:** | | |
| S1 | Describe and define general developmental, academic, social, career, and functional characteristics of individuals who would benefit most from a independent curriculum as they relate to levels of support needed. | |
| **IC: 3.** | **Independence Curriculum Assessment, Diagnosis, and Evaluation** | |
| **Knowledge:** | | |
| K1 | Specialized terminology used in the assessment of individuals who would benefit most from a functional independence curriculum as they relate to levels of support needed. | |
| K2 | Legal provisions, regulations, and guidelines regarding unbiased assessment and use of psychometric instruments and instructional assessment measures with individuals with disabilities* as they relate to levels of support needed. | |
| K3 | Specialized policies regarding screening, referral, and placement procedures for individuals who would benefit most from a functional independence curriculum as they relate to levels of support needed. | |
| **Skills:** | | |
| S1 | Implement procedures for assessing and reporting both appropriate and problematic social behaviors of individuals with disabilities*. | |
| S2 | Use exceptionality-specific assessment instruments with individuals with disabilities*. | |
| S3 | Adapt and modify existing assessment tools and methods to accommodate the unique abilities and needs of individuals who would benefit most from a functional independence curriculum. | |
| S4 | Develop and use a technology plan based on adaptive technology assessment. | |

| | Guidelines | Cite the course number and/or course lecture or activity in which each standard was mastered. |
|---|---|---|
| S5 | Assess reliable method(s) of response of individuals who lack typical communication and performance abilities. | |
| **IC:** **4.** | **Independence Curriculum** **Instructional Content and Practice** | |
| *Knowledge:* | | |
| K1 | The sources of specialized materials, equipment, and assistive technology for individuals with disabilities*. | |
| K2 | The impact of language development on the academic and social skills of individuals with disabilities*. | |
| K3 | The impact of disabilities on auditory skills of individuals with disabilities*. | |
| K4 | The impact of social skills on the lives of individuals with disabilities*. | |
| *Skills:* | | |
| S1 | Facilitate use of prevention and intervention strategies in educational settings. | |
| S2 | Use technology including assistive devices. | |
| S3 | Use reinforcement systems to create effective learning environments. | |
| S4 | Use student-initiated learning experiences and integrate them into ongoing instruction. | |
| S5 | Use effective instructional strategies to assist individuals with disabilities* to detect and correct errors in oral and written language. | |
| S6 | Choose appropriate methods and instructional strategies according to the characteristics of the learner. | |
| S7 | Design and implement sensory stimulation programs. | |
| S8 | Teach culturally responsive functional life skills. | |
| S9 | Use research-supported instructional strategies and practices. | |
| S10 | Design age-appropriate instruction based on the adaptive skills of learners. | |
| S11 | Integrate related services into the instructional settings of learners. | |
| S12 | Provide community referenced and community based instruction. | |

| | Guidelines | *Cite the course number and/or course lecture or activity in which each standard was mastered.* |
|---|---|---|
| S13 | Assist students in the use of alternative and augmentative communication systems. | |
| S14 | Use appropriate physical management techniques, including positioning, handling, lifting, relaxation, and range of motion. | |
| S15 | Facilitate learner's use of orthotic, prosthetic, and adaptive equipment. | |
| S16 | Select and use media, materials, and resources required with learners whose disabilities interfere with communications. | |
| S17 | Interpret sensory, mobility, reflex, and perceptual information to create appropriate learning plans. | |
| S18 | Use appropriate adaptations and assistive technology. | |
| S19 | Adapt lessons that minimize the physical exertion of individuals with specialized health care. | |
| S20 | Design and implement instructional programs that address functional independence skills emphasizing positive self-concepts and realistic goals. | |
| S21 | Design and implement strategies for medical self-management procedures. | |
| S22 | Participate in the selection and implementation of augmentative or alternative communication devices and systems. | |
| **IC: 5.** | **Independence Curriculum Planning and Managing the Teaching and Learning Environment** | |
| *Knowledge:* | | |
| K1 | Model career, vocational, and transition programs for individuals with disabilities* who are most likely to make progress in a functional independence curriculum. | |
| K2 | Issues, resources, and techniques used to integrate students in a functional independence curriculum into and out of alternative environments, including special centers, psychiatric hospitals, and residential treatment centers. | |
| K3 | Appropriate use of assistive devices to meet the needs of individuals with disabilities*. | |
| K4 | Specialized health care practices, first-aid techniques, and other medically relevant | |

| | Guidelines | Cite the course number and/or course lecture or activity in which each standard was mastered. |
|---|---|---|
| | interventions necessary to maintain the health and safety of individuals with disabilities in a variety of educational settings. | |
| K5 | Common environmental and personal barriers that hinder accessibility and acceptance of individuals with disabilities*. | |
| **Skills:** | | |
| S1 | Monitor intragroup behavior changes across subjects and activities. | |
| S2 | Structure the educational environment for optimal learning opportunities. | |
| S3 | Teach individuals with disabilities who are in a functional independence curriculum in a variety of settings. | |
| S4 | Design learning environments that provides feedback from peers and adults. | |
| S5 | Design learning environments that are multisensory and that facilitate active participation, self-advocacy, and independence of individuals with disabilities* in a variety of group and individual learning activities. | |
| S6 | Use local, community, state, and provincial resources to assist in programming. | |
| S7 | Coordinate activities of related services personnel to maximize direct instruction time for individuals with disabilities* who are studying an individualized independence curriculum. | |
| S8 | Use techniques of physical positioning and management of individuals with physical and health disabilities to ensure participation in academic and social environments. | |
| S9 | Demonstrate appropriate body mechanics to ensure student and teacher safety in transfer, lifting, positioning, and seating. | |
| S10 | Use appropriate adaptive equipment such as wedges, seat inserts, and standers to facilitate positioning, mobility, communication, and learning for individuals with physical and health disabilities. | |
| S11 | Use positioning techniques that decrease inappropriate tone and facilitate appropriate postural reactions to enhance participation. | |

| Guidelines | Cite the course number and/or course lecture or activity in which each standard was mastered. |
|---|---|
| **IC: Independence Curriculum**<br>**6. Managing Student Behavior and Social Interaction Skills** | |
| *Knowledge:* | |
| K1 | Rationale for selecting specific management techniques for individuals with disabilities*. | |
| K2 | Continuum of alternative placements and programs available to individuals with disabilities*; state, provincial, and local services available; and the advantages and disadvantages of placement options and programs within the continuum of services. | |
| K3 | Theories behind reinforcement techniques and their applications for teaching individuals with disabilities*. | |
| K4 | Theories of behavior problems in individuals with disabilities*, including self-stimulation and self-abuse. | |
| K5 | Impact of multiple disabilities on behavior and learning. | |
| K6 | Communication and social interaction alternatives for individuals who are nonspeaking. | |
| *Skills:* | |
| S1 | Use a variety of nonaversive techniques for the purpose of controlling targeted behavior and maintaining attention of individuals with disabilities*. | |
| S2 | Develop and implement systematic behavior management plans for individuals with disabilities* using observation, recording, charting, timelines, intervention hierarchies, and schedules of reinforcement. | |
| S3 | Select target behaviors to be changed and identify the critical variables affecting the target behavior. | |
| S4 | Define and use skills in problem-solving and conflict resolution. | |
| S5 | Design, implement, and evaluate instructional programs that enhance the individual's social participation in family, school, and community activities. | |
| S6 | Develop and facilitate use of behavior crisis management plans. | |

| | Guidelines | Cite the course number and/or course lecture or activity in which each standard was mastered. |
|---|---|---|
| S7 | Facilitate development and implementation of rules and appropriate consequences. | |
| **IC:**<br>**7.** | **Independence Curriculum**<br>**Communication and Collaborative**<br>**Partnerships** | |
| *Knowledge:* | | |
| K1 | Sources of unique services, networks, and organizations for individuals with disabilities*, including career, vocational, and transition support. | |
| K2 | Parent education programs and behavior management guides, including those commercially available, that address the management of severe behavioral problems and facilitate communication links applicable to individuals with disabilities*. | |
| K3 | Collaborative and/or consultative roles of the special education teachers and paraeducators in the integration of individuals with disabilities* into general classrooms. | |
| K4 | Types and importance of information generally available from family, school officials, legal system, community service agencies. | |
| K5 | Roles and responsibilities of school-based medical and related services personnel, professional groups, and community organizations in identifying, assessing, and providing services to individuals with disabilities*. | |
| *Skills:* | | |
| S1 | Assist students, in collaboration with parents and other professionals, in planning for transition to adulthood including employment, community, and daily life, with maximum opportunities for decision making and full participation in the community. | |
| S2 | Use strategies to work with chronically ill and terminally ill individuals and their families. | |
| **IC:**<br>**8.** | **Independence Curriculum**<br>**Professionalism and Ethical Practices** | |
| *Knowledge:* | | |
| K1 | Consumer and professional organizations, publications, and journals relevant to individuals | |

| Guidelines | Cite the course number and/or course lecture or activity in which each standard was mastered. |
|---|---|
| with disabilities*. | |
| K2 Rights to privacy, confidentiality, and respect for differences among all persons interacting with individuals with disabilities*. | |
| K3 Types and transmission routes of infectious disease. | |
| *Skills:* | |
| S1 Participate in the activities of professional organizations relevant to individuals with disabilities*. | |
| S2 Articulate the teacher's ethical responsibility to individuals who function similarly to individuals with disabilities* (e.g., individuals at risk). | |
| S3 Seek information regarding protocols, procedural guidelines, and policies designed to assist individuals with disabilities* as they participate in school and community-based activities. | |
| S4 Maintain confidentiality of medical and academic records and respect for privacy of individuals with disabilities*. | |

*Implicit to all of the knowledge and skills standards in this section is the focus on individuals with disabilities whose education is in an individualized independence curriculum.